When he was a child, David was

His father, a canny Scot, gla

asked, 'Is that your good shoes y

When David replied in the affirmative, his father retorted, 'well, take bigger steps then!'

The lesson was not lost on David. So when it came to undertaking the Walk for Wallace in August 2005, where David followed the footsteps of Wallace's final journey from Robroyston near Glasgow to London to commemorate the murder of Scotland's patriot hero (see his book *For Freedom*), he recalled his father's words.

David had the genius to devise a pair of built up shoes so that he actually took many fewer steps than he should have, on the long journey south.

People continue to believe he is six foot five, the shoes notwithstanding, and he continues to ride round his beloved Scotland on a large motorcycle (mainly because he would look even stupider on a small one) looking for the wee out of the way places where the deeds that make up our chequered history took place.

The one drawback about being a patriot who often wears a kilt or plaid to events, is that it is difficult to hide specially designed footwear while dressed in that garb, and he is scared people will start to notice the join.

By the same author:

Desire Lines: A Scottish Odyssey
For Freedom
A Passion for Scotland
On the Trail of Bonnie Prince Charlie
On the Trail of Robert the Bruce
On the Trail of William Wallace

Also available in Luath's *On the Trail of* series:

On the Trail of Scotland's History

To Linda

Best Wishes

DAVID R. ROSS

David R Ross
Dumfries
Aug 2009

Luath Press Limited

EDINBURGH

www.luath.co.uk

First Published 2007

ISBN (10): 1-905222-85-8
ISBN (13): 978-1-9-0522285-8

The author's right to be identified as author of this book under the
Copyright, Designs and Patents Act 1988 has been asserted.

The paper used in this book is recyclable. It is made from
low-chlorine pulps produced in a low-energy, low-emission
manner from renewable forests.

Printed and bound by
Scotprint, Haddington

Typeset in 10.5 point Sabon by
3btype.com

Contents

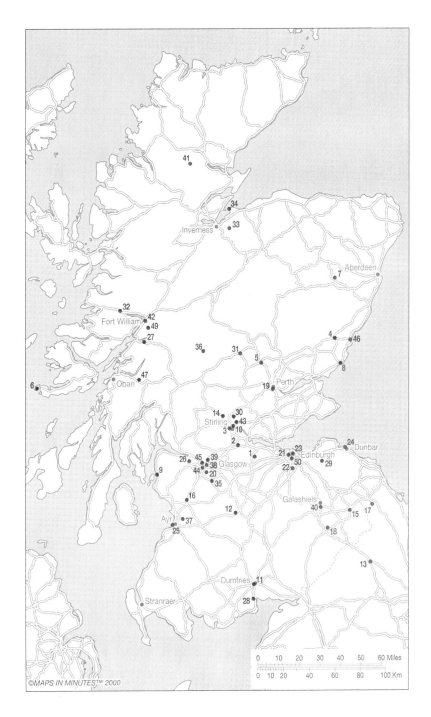

41

34
Inverness 33

Aberdeen
7

32
42
Fort William 49
27
36 31
5
47 19 Perth
Oban
6

14 30
Stirling 43
3 10
2
1
26 45 39 23 24 Dunbar
38 21 Edinburgh
44 20 Glasgow 22 50 29
35
9
16
12 Galashiels
40
Ayr 37 15 17
25 18

13

Dumfries 11
Stranraer 28

0   10   20   30   40   50   60 Miles
0 10 20   40   60   80   100 Km

©MAPS IN MINUTES™ 2000

viii

Key to Map

CHAPTER ONE

In ancestral footsteps

Stone has always been a magical substance in Scotland.

I SUPPOSE FEW OF US give a second thought to our earliest ancestors, the folk who first colonised 'Scotland' after the last ice age, but their blood runs in the veins of many modern Scots and remnants of their times dot our landscape.

Our forefathers used stone, always in plentiful supply, to build their memorials, their burial mounds and their cairns. Stone has always been a magical substance in Scotland – the legends surrounding the Stone of Destiny testify to that, and the early peoples went to great effort, dragging huge monoliths many miles, or stones in their thousands to high hilltops, to take their place in shaping our history by building their cairns and temples.

When thinking of these stone memorials, we tend to immediately focus on the impressive Highlands and Islands examples, like Callanish stone circle on the Island of Lewis, or the Ring of Brodgar in Orkney. It is true the finest examples are in the less industrialised parts of Scotland. In fact, that is the very reason for their survival. People used the stones gathered for burial cairns as a handy source of material in later centuries, so the ones which stand the furthest from densely populated areas have had more chance of survival.

However, there are still some sites well worth a visit in the heavily populated Central Belt.

Cairnpapple Hill is not only an easily accessible example, lying just a few miles north of the M8, but it is also a fabulous viewpoint on a clear day. It stands near the village of Torphichen in West Lothian with views stretching as far as Arran to the west and the Bass Rock to the east. Its summit boasts a large burial cairn surrounded by earthworks and burial pits. You park, and there is an easy walk over the last few hundred yards to the hill's summit. There is a little visitor centre, and you can climb inside the refurbished centre of the main burial mound, where there are ancient graves within.

Many hills have remains of large cairns on their summits; they are comprised of thousands, if not millions, of stones that must have taken a phenomenal number of man-hours to gather and carry to the hilltops to construct. Two fine examples are Tinto Hill near Lanark, and Cairntable above Muirkirk in Ayrshire.

One of the most accessible sites in central Scotland is Huly Hill, which stands just a few yards west of Newbridge roundabout, where the M8 and M9 join. Standing 30 metres across and three metres high, it was once large stone circle, but now only three of the stones remain, although there is a large outlying stone to the right at the Edinburgh side of the roundabout, just a few feet inside the surrounding fence of a factory. Motorists pass within feet of it daily without realizing it exists.

Talking of driving, nearly all Scotland's major through-routes follow the same lines our stone-age ancestors used, for the hilly topography of our country dictates few route choices between two points.

An examination of any Ordnance Survey map will reveal ancient sites scattered over the face of the land.

I cover the countryside on a regular basis and am always amazed at the standing stones I come across by accident. Carrying a map will reveal many others, some close to smaller roads where you can park and examine them.

The North East is particularly rich in ancient stone remains. Many standing stones have been used for later purposes than those for which they were erected. Some have been carved with Christian symbols.

The Wallace Stones near the Sheriffmuir Inn on a shoulder of the Ochil Hills (they are marked on Ordnance Survey maps) are ancient monoliths, but they may have been used as a gathering site for part of the army before the Battle of Stirling Bridge in 1297. The Scots were led by Wallace, and so the name has stuck. They were possibly raised by the dwellers of the hill fort on nearby Dumyat.

Two standing stones at Randolphfield police headquarters in Stirling were used by one of the Scots Divisions as a marker line at the Battle of Bannockburn. They lined up at these two standing stones to withstand an English cavalry charge.

So we can see our medieval counterparts also used the stones erected by their ancestors as landmarks. Many of the islands off our shores have remains in a good state of preservation. Arran has several well-preserved stone circles.

There is much controversy surrounding the exact purpose of our standing stones and circles. It would seem that many may have been used as calculators or calendars, and special places where sky deities were worshipped. Later, they became sought-after burial sites.

The ancient peoples also built circles from wood, which time has eroded, although we can still locate the pits that served as foundations for the wooden posts. This leaves only the stones and cairns standing in mute testament to the existence of our forefathers.

CHAPTER TWO

The legacy of Rome's north-west frontier

Throughout history, no one has ever managed to gain rule of Scotland by armed invasion.

WHEN THE ROMAN EMPEROR HADRIAN visited Britain in AD 121 he ordered the building of the wall, from the Solway to the Tyne, which carries his name.

Although none of Hadrian's Wall is in modern Scotland, it is still seen as a psychological barrier between Scotland and England.

Many long stretches of it are intact, and the more interesting parts are well signposted, with information boards. The best-preserved stretch runs a little north of Brampton, eastwards to the area north of Hexham.

It is easy to stand atop this stonework and look north over the rolling moorland towards Scotland, as many a Roman legionary, used to much warmer climes, must have done, while keeping an eye open for the warlike Caledonians.

20 years after the building of Hadrian's Wall, a push northwards was made to the narrow waist of land between the Forth and Clyde. Here the Antonine Wall, an earthen structure defended by a deep ditch, looking north to the Campsies and Ochils, was built.

Several stretches of the Antonine Wall exist in a reasonable condition, and are well worth visiting for a chance to marvel at the tenacity of the Roman builders.

The later Forth and Clyde Canal follows the same basic route as the Antonine Wall, and near it, on the stretch between Castlecary and Falkirk, via Bonnybridge, are sites such as Rough Castle and Seabegs Wood. These are signposted from nearby roads.

Rough Castle has an interesting surviving defensive feature, a series of dug pits in clusters, known as *lillia*, designed to break up a charge and probably originally containing sharpened stakes. The stretch of the Antonine here is probably the best-preserved section, the ditch and earthen rampart still relatively unscathed.

A remnant of the stone base of the wall is visible in New Kilpatrick cemetery in the Bearsden and Milngavie area.

The Romans also built a supply port for shipping at Cramond at the wall's eastern end, where in recent years a carved stone lioness was found in the River Almond. This lioness is now on display at the Museum of Scotland in Edinburgh.

Two main routes ran north to the Antonine Wall. One followed the line of the A68 through Lauderdale, and north over the Lammermuirs at Soutra, a line later used by many invading English armies. The other followed a route similar to the modern M74/A74, threading up Annandale, and over into Clydesdale.

But all the backbreaking work of the Romans was to no avail. Around AD 160, the Romans abandoned the Antonine Wall, moving back to Hadrian's Wall, holding it for another hundred years until the empire began to decline. I often wonder how the average Roman soldier felt as they marched off south. All the work that went into building the wall, its supply roads, its forts, and then after a few years it was abandoned.

There had been forays north of the Antonine, of course – there is that abiding legend that Pontius Pilate was born at Fortingall in Perthshire, where stands an ancient yew, said to pre-date Roman times; the suggestion being that Pilate himself would have been familiar with this tree. In fact, I have seen it claimed that the famous Fortingall Yew is the oldest living thing in Europe! This tree is a fragment of what it once was in its prime though. Much of it is rotted away and only a few boughs are still living.

Many forts and sites scattered over southern Scotland can be found on Ordnance Survey maps. Strathclyde Park has an excavated bathhouse, which stands on the bank of the South Calder, where it enters the man-made loch. Enough remains to discern how warm air was allowed to flow underneath the flooring. Early central heating!

A well-defined rampart and ditch can be seen above the A72 west of Peebles, some 500 metres west of Lyne Church. It is just above the road, but unless you knew of its whereabouts you would not know it was so close to you as you drove this stretch. It was the base of a cohort of cavalry and the sheer size of scale leaves one in no doubt as to the power wielded during the days of the Roman occupation of Scotland.

Throughout history, despite numerous attempts, no one has ever managed to subjugate Scotland by armed invasion.

Politics may have been another force to be reckoned with in the centuries to come, but when all of Europe had finally bowed to Roman conquest, Scotland alone was able to hold off against what must have seemed to be relentless attacks and overwhelming odds.

CHAPTER THREE

On the trail of the Camelot legend

King Arthur's legendary exploits could have taken place in Scotland.

ONE OF THE OLDEST and most abiding British legends is the story of King Arthur and his Knights of the Round Table. Over the years the story has been credited as having its roots in south-western England, but there is a case for Arthur's exploits having taken place in Scotland. It may all be legend, but the arguments surrounding it can be good fun.

Arthur was King of the Britons, and the Britons had their headquarters at Dun Breatann (the fort of the Britons), or Dumbarton as we know it today. Or it refers more specifically to the castle on Dumbarton Rock, which has borne a fortification on its summit since earliest times.

Arthur was said to have been active in the 6th century and this time fits the theory that he was one of the leaders of the Strathclyde Britons based at Dun Breatann.

To add a little more weight to a Scottish background for Arthur, the town is called Castrum Arthuri (Arthur's Castle) in a record of David II from 1367. David would have been very familiar with this area, as he was raised by his father, Robert the Bruce, in a house on the banks of the River Leven, within a mile or so of Dumbarton Rock itself, and so he was perhaps regaled with Arthurian tales as a lad. Dumbarton Castle is open to the public, and although it is mostly a shell of its former glories, it is worth a visit just to climb to the summit of either of its twin peaks and look at the phenomenal views over the Clyde and the Leven.

Camelon, on the outskirts of Falkirk, has been identified with Camelot; not as bizarre a claim as this might at first seem. The Romans had founded a town here as a base for the running of the northern boundary of their empire, at the Antonine Wall. After the Roman influence declined, it is more than likely that the natives would have used it as a fortification of their own, including perhaps Arthur himself.

We have, of course, the famous Arthur's Seat in Edinburgh, and Ben Arthur, a mountain at the head of Loch Long, which is better known as the Cobbler. Unfortunately, these names have been derived from some long-lost connection.

Drummelzier, in south-west Peeblesshire, is reputed to be the burial place of Merlin, the magician whose story is intertwined with that of Arthur. Merlin's grave is sited at the side of the Powsail Burn, which flows into the Tweed some quarter of a mile after running through Drummelzier itself. In a description of Tweedale published in 1715, it is stated that Merlin was buried beneath a thorn tree, a little below the churchyard.

The thorn tree is long gone, but it is interesting to walk the Powsail down to the Tweed, and speculate on the exact location of the final resting place of the world's most famous sorcerer.

A mound in the graveyard at Meigle in Perthshire has long been pointed out as Vanora's Grave. Our ancestors knew Guinevere, Arthur's wife in the old legends, as Vanora. The stone that once graced this mound is now in the little sculptured stone museum that is adjacent to the churchyard.

One of my personal favourites is the legend concerning the Round Table itself. On the level grassland below Stirling Castle there is a strange symmetrical and angled mound known locally as The King's Knot. It stands just beside Dumbarton Road. The information boards nearby date it to the time of the Stewart dynasty in Scotland, but a poem written in 1370 by John Barbour mentions 'The Round Table' and there is no doubt that it is this strange construction he is referring to. Barbour tells how, after the Battle of Bannockburn, King Edward II of England had to make a getaway by travelling by 'The Round Table' to escape the clutches of the victorious Scots.

The King's Knot has ramps on its sides, which knights on horseback could easily have ridden up in order to stand in a circle on the summit. There is a centre boss where Arthur could have stood to give and receive counselling. It is certainly a poignant place to visit and walk over, but the best views of it can be had from the ramparts of Stirling Castle, high above.

CHAPTER FOUR

Evidence of the Norse age

The badge on Rover cars is a daily reminder of Vikings.

FOR FOUR CENTURIES, the Vikings occupied the islands and parts of mainland Scotland, before their power was broken here in the mid–1200s. Their legacy has survived, however, not only in the blonde hair and blue eyes of many of the people of Scotland's western seaboard, but also in place names.

Skye, for instance, takes its name from the Norse *Skuyî* – the Cloud Island – which is how they saw the cloud-capped peaks from the sea.

The north-western point of the mainland, Cape Wrath, takes its name from the Norse *Hvarf* – the turning point – where their ships would turn their prows south to sail through the Hebrides.

What few remnants we have from Viking times generally lie close to water, as the Norsemen did not like to roam far from their ships.

Many Glaswegians would be surprised to know that Govan, on the south bank of the Clyde, was a Viking settlement. Various arte-facts have been found here, including Viking hogback tombstones, which are shaped like the keels of upturned boats. These have been moved inside Govan Parish Church for safekeeping.

It's strange to think that places where dragon-prowed longships were once drawn up on the banks, where their fierce axe-carrying crews waded ashore, later became the sites of shipyards. Even odder to think that these too have almost vanished, but that one of the few names left on the Clyde is Kvaerner – a Scandinavian company.

Apart from the five hogback Viking tombstones in Govan Old Parish Church, I have only ever once come across another hogback-style tombstone well away from the sea – by the entrance to the 1655 church in the village of Dalserf, just south of the Garrion Bridge over the Clyde between Hamilton and Lanark.

How did a Viking-style burial stone come to be situated so far from the open sea? Perhaps the Clyde this far upstream was once navigable for shallow-draughted longships.

There are also two remaining ancient round towers in Scotland, built by Celtic monks as a defence against Viking raiders. One is at Brechin, now adjoined to the later cathedral. The other fine example is in the village of Abernethy, just south of the Tay. A circular stair takes you up to the summit trap door, where you have a bird's eye view over the village and surrounding country, allowing you to cast your mind back to when Viking marauders rampaged across the land.

There are many earthworks scattered over Scotland's countryside that locals, or at least old local histories, refer to as 'Danish Forts'.

One of these is in the Devilla Forest, north of the A985, which runs from the Kincardine Bridge to Dunfermline. It is marked on Ordnance Survey maps. Just a little north-west of the farm of Bordie stands the Standard Stone. This flat stone has a socket carved into it, and it was said to have been where the standard of an army was displayed during a battle between the Vikings and the Scots, the Vikings having sailed up the Firth of Forth, only a mile south.

Viking rule in Scotland was broken firstly by Somerled, the ancestor of the Lords of the Isles, who, with his own long ships, beat the Vikings at their own game. He died in battle at Renfrew and is buried at Saddell Abbey in Kintyre.

Next to help break the Viking hold was King Alexander III of Scots, who defeated the King of Norway at the Battle of Largs in 1263. There is a monument at the south end of Largs, known as the Pencil, which commemorates this victory. Largs also has the modern exhibition Vikingar, recalling the area's links with the Norse raiders.

The leader of the Vikings at the Battle of Largs was King Haakon, and Kyleakin (*Kyle Haakon*) on the Isle of Skye opposite Kyle of Lochalsh takes its name from him, as the Viking fleet berthed there before sailing south to defeat at Largs.

CHAPTER FIVE

Scotland's early kings

The Gaels' moving power base is tracked.

WHEN THE GAELS founded their kingdom of Dál Riata – now modern Argyll – Dunadd was their capital. It is a prime spot, rising out of the Mhoine Mhor – the Great Moss – an extensive area of flat ground which would give defenders early warning of a body of men approaching.

Dunadd can still be visited and is signposted from the village of Kilmichael, a couple of miles north of the Crinan Canal. A few tumbledown stones are all that remain of the old fortifications, but there are other artefacts worth viewing.

As you enter the fort, you walk through a passage in the rock into what was originally the lower defensive area. Climbing higher, you find the remains of a stairway leading up to the second defensive area. It is on the summit that some fascinating features remain. On one stone is the imprinted carving of a human foot.

This would have been used in some kind of inauguration ceremony. The people coming to take oaths to the king could carry some of their own soil and pour it into the footprint, to swear fealty while standing on their own 'land'. Or perhaps the king himself placed his foot into the carving, to symbolise his relationship with his kingdom's living rock.

The act does not seem so bizarre when you consider that it was – according to legend – at Dunadd that the Stone of Destiny was kept when it was first brought to Scotland from Ireland, to act as the throne of the King of Scots during the crowning ceremonies. Stone had an important part to play in the ceremonies of our ancestors.

Also on the hilltop can be seen the outline of a wild boar. This carving faces that of the foot. The wild boar was the badge of the

King of Scots until the time of William I, who changed his standard to that of a rampant lion, the symbol we still know today.

The area surrounding Dunadd is full of early Scottish artefacts. A little north at Nether Largie are several old burial cairns, the most impressive of which is known as South Cairn. Nearby stands the Templewood stone circle, where eight standing stones surround a central monolith. Just to the north is Kilmartin village, in whose churchyard can be found a fine collection of carved stones. There are the two early-Christian Kilmartin crosses, and sculptured stones and gravestones of the Malcolm family, showing effigies of knights in armour.

It was Kenneth MacAlpin who moved the Gaels' power base eastward from Dunadd to the area surrounding Scone and Forteviot. Scone became famous as the place where Scots kings were crowned, and although it is centuries since such a coronation, the Moot Hill, where the crownings took place, stands in mute testament of those times. It is in the grounds of the later Scone Palace.

It is said that Kenneth MacAlpin was present at the Battle of Athelstaneford, which gave birth to Scotland's flag. At this battle, a huge white cross appeared across the blue summer sky, and the Picts took this omen – the cross of St Andrew – as a sign of forthcoming victory. St Andrew was crucified on an x-shaped cross, and it was taken as a sign that God was on their side. The battle was won and the Picts and Scots adopted the sign as the symbol for their nation – it is the oldest flag in the world still in use.

The village of Athelstaneford stands a little north of the AI at Haddington in East Lothian. Behind the church a little doocot has been turned into a visitor centre, and a nearby plaque states, 'here was the flag of Scotland born'. You can stand and look out towards the Peffer Burn as our ancestors did on that fateful day, when our future flag was seen as a symbol in the sky.

MacAlpin transferred his capital from Dunadd to Forteviot, now a modern village six miles south-west of Perth. His headquarters stood on an eminence, now called the Halyhill, at the west end of the village.

One old chronicle said: 'First to reign in Albany, 'tis said was Kenneth son of Alpin, warrior bold. He expelled the Picts, reigned twice eight years and in Forteviot met his death.' Another stated that Kenneth 'died of a tumour on the ides of February, the third day of the week, in the palace of Forteviot.'

He was taken to Iona to join many of his ancestors in the burial ground of the kings. Many slabs or gravestones still lie there, and although we do not know to which king each of these eroded grave markers was ascribed, one is definitely that of MacAlpin.

Very little structural work remains from the time of MacAlpin, but he has one lasting legacy in the Cathedral at Dunkeld. Although the church is said to have been founded by Constantine, King of the Picts, MacAlpin is credited with its completion. He transferred some relics of St Columba here from Iona to protect them from Viking raids. The Apostle's Stone in the cathedral may depict Columba.

Various versions of this holy building have come and gone, but it still stands proud in Dunkeld, and as Kenneth is credited with much shedding of blood in the old chronicles, it is strange that a religious establishment is one of the few relics of his reign.

CHAPTER SIX

The warriors' resting place

The haven where battling kings found peace.

FOR 200 YEARS AFTER the death of Kenneth MacAlpin in 858, kings came and kings went, most of them going in a very bloody and violent way indeed.

To take just three, Malcolm I met his end in combat; his successor Indulf was another battle statistic; and the next man in was King Dub or Dubh, the Gaelic for black, a name he lived up to – or died up to – in a very strange way. But more anon of this terrible trio.

What's interesting today as we travel round Scotland, with one eye on scenery and one on our history, is the scatter of places where our kings met their untimely ends. Some of them were slain in battle, like Kenneth III and his son Giric II, who not only reigned together, but also died together in battle at Strathearn in 1005. Some kings received injuries that later killed them, like Malcolm II, who won a mighty victory over the English at Carham, near Coldstream on the River Tweed. He was still fighting in 1034, when, at the age of 80, he received a wound that killed him several days later, in Glamis. There is a carved standing stone in the garden of the manse in Glamis that may have a connection to this affair. A few kings died in simple cases of assassination by those who wanted to be next in line for the throne. One such was Donald III, captured by his successor Edgar, who put out his eyes before killing him at Rescobie, near Forfar, in 1097. Looking through the chronicles, we find very few of our monarchs died in a peaceable way!

One thing these kings all had in common was that they were buried in Iona. Even those who had been slain by enemies were still granted burial on the holy isle. The sanctity of Iona as a last resting place for those with royal blood seems to have been more important than the feuds that royal blood could cause.

So to Iona, the most widely known connection to the Scotland of a previous millennium. Let's take the ferry from Oban; or from Fionnphort on Mull, over the mile or so of sea to the little holy isle, famous for its abbey and for being the last resting place of so many early Scots kings.

The old burial ground, known as the *Relig Oran*, is said to provide a final peace for no fewer than 48 of these royals. Also four kings of Ireland and eight from Norway. Iona is a scenic island in its own right. But add its reputation for bestowing tranquillity on the living as well as on the dead; add its starring role in our nation's history, and its lure is surely irresistible.

Before or after we go island hopping, we can take a little time-out, on the shores of Loch Feochan, beside the A816, south of Oban. A mile or so short of Kilninver, take a look at the natural rock strand running along the shore. In the mist of lost centuries, in the days before MacBrayne ruled the waves, this rock was where ships left for Iona with the bodies of our kings, en route to their ultimate destination. It is called *Creag na Marbh*, the Rock of the Dead. It is thought that some ships left from Corpach by Fort William too, as *Corpach* is the Gaelic for Place of the Dead.

Now to a king who took a rather circuitous route to the holy isle, if indeed he got there at all. Constantine II is our man, the first of Kenneth MacAlpin's descendants to be buried somewhere other than Iona.

He was very much the exception to the rule during these violent times, surviving more than 40 years after being crowned, and finally bowing out with what the old chronicles call the straw death, meaning that he died in bed rather than battle.

What improved his life expectancy was that Constantine abdicated and became a monk at St Andrews. The church where he served was probably incorporated within the later cathedral, now itself a ruin. And no visitor to St Andrews should miss the cathedral: the remaining fragments still give us a wonderful glimpse of past glories.

St Andrews is the likely site of Constantine's original burial, but legend tells us that monks from Iona later exhumed their brother's body and took him to the *Relig Oran* to rest alongside his ancestors.

Constantine II's successor – and this is where we began today's story – was Malcolm I, who was slain in battle at Fetteresso, just inland from Stonehaven and Dunnottar Castle, in 954. After Malcolm came Indulf, killed in battle where the Deskford Burn meets the sea at Cullen in Banffshire, in 962. Both were buried at Iona, as was the black-haired Dub or Dubh – eventually.

But what a strange story, repeated in every surviving early chronicle, springs from Dubh's death in battle at Forres. According to these reports, no sooner was Dubh buried by his killers, a little way north, under a bridge crossing the Kinloss Burn, than... the sun failed to rise. From that moment on, old Sol would not appear and darkness covered Scotland. This darkness, say the chronicles, continued while Dubh's men searched for his body, and only when it had been found, and carried 180 miles to Iona did the light return.

One rational explanation is that there had been a volcanic eruption somewhere, and the ensuing ash cloud blocked out the sun. But who wants to be rational when there is such a good story to tell? What is also interesting is that there is a carving of a bridge on Sueno's Stone, a mighty standing stone in Forres, only a couple of miles distant from the scene of the battle where Dubh was slain. One of the figures on the stone is said to be Dubh, and the stone carries a battle scene. It stands 23 feet high, and I'm told there is another 12 feet underground. It is the tallest carven standing stone in Scotland, and though it has been caged in a glass screen to preserve it, I think that this does not detract from its magnificence.

CHAPTER SEVEN

Final curtain for Macbeth

The last battleground of a Scots king who captured world attention.

WILLIAM SHAKESPEARE may have immortalised Macbeth, but his story owes more to the imagination than fact.

The playwright did, however, agree with legend on the site of Macbeth's fortress. This was on Dunsinnan Hill, one of the Sidlaw Hills, which stands eight miles north-east of Perth.

Macbeth was afforded useful views over Strathmore and Blairgowrie from his conical style battle station. A place where approaching enemies would be spied from afar.

The hill on which his stronghold sat rises 600ft – gradually on its north-west side and more steeply on its other sides, making it difficult for an attacking force to gain access. The remains of the ancient fort can still be seen.

A rampart and ditches running around the upper part of the hill defended the king's fortress, 210ft long by 130ft wide. There have been various archaeological digs over the years, which have uncovered various bits and pieces, but, if legend is correct, the greatest item has still to be found.

According to the stories handed down through generations, the 'real' Stone of Destiny is somewhere hidden within the hill.

There are several versions to the tale, but all have the same theme. When Edward I, 'Longshanks', invaded Scotland in 1296, he stole the various talismen of the Scottish people, including the famous stone on which the Scots kings were crowned. He did this in the belief that it would give him some sort of right of rule over the northern kingdom.

It has always been stated that the abbot at Scone, where the stone was kept, would not have been so naive as to let it slip into

Edward's clutches, and must have substituted a copy. All legend, but it was reported that on 19 November 1819, a vault was found beneath the soil of Dunsinnan Hill that contained a carved marble stone, which was believed to be the true stone, hidden in 1296 from English hands. More believable because the hill is not too far from Scone, so perhaps this is the place where the abbot decided to hide the Stone from grasping English hands...

This story has been repeated over the years: People are out on the hill, where they discover a crack in the rock, or where an opening has been created by a small landslide, and the stone is found within, but the discoverers are unable to find the opening again when returning with others, or another landslide has covered the hole. If anyone discovers the stone while on a visit to the hill, I'd love to hear from them!

Dunsinnan Hill stands near the village of Collace, a little south of the A94, which runs from New Scone to Coupar Angus. Shakespeare had Macbeth's end come when Birnam Wood marched to Dunsinnan. The original ancient forest in the Dunkeld area has gone, all except one ancient gnarled specimen, signposted as being the last of the Birnam Oaks; but careful landowners have planted swathes of fir and birch over the last two centuries, so Birnam Wood in a way survives, with the little village of Birnam at its core.

Birnam sits at the side of the A9, a little south of Dunkeld. Interestingly, there is an old hill-fort on Birnam Hill, slightly south of the village, which is pointed out as 'Duncan's Camp' – a reference to King Duncan, slain by Macbeth before he assumed the crown.

Birnam Hill is 1,324ft high, and the hill-fort ascribed to Duncan stands at an altitude of 658ft on its south-eastern side. It is worth remembering that the armies of both Montrose and Bonnie Prince Charlie poured into the Lowlands through the pass here at Birnam.

The real location of Macbeth's death is Lumphanan, which stands 25 miles west of Aberdeen, on the A980, between Banchory and Alford. His end came after he had been pursued over the Mounth, the great range of hills that separates Deeside from the glens further south, by his successor, Malcolm Canmore, son of King Duncan.

The site of Macbeth's death is said to be on Perk Hill, about one mile north by west of the parish church. The cairn, which is said to mark the spot, was described in 1793 as '40 yards in circumference and pretty high up in the middle'.

Macbeth's body – as Duncan's had been – was interred on the island of Iona, among the bones of many of his ancestors.

CHAPTER EIGHT

The Lion sets a new Standard

The last traces of two Scots kings.

WILLIAM I OF SCOTLAND is generally referred to as 'The Lion' in our history books. Not because he was any great shakes as a warrior, but because he was the first to use the 'Lion Rampant' as his standard – the same emblem so beloved by Scottish crowds at modern sporting events.

The story goes that he was gifted a couple of lions by some wealthy individual returning from a crusade, and kept them as pets at Stirling Castle. Indeed, there is still a part of the castle known as the Lions' Den. William liked these roaring beasts so much that he had one depicted, standing upright, and claws raking, on his armourial bearings. Every King and Queen of Scots has used it since.

William had a long, fairly uneventful reign, but he has left a lasting legacy by being the founder of the Abbey of Arbroath.

It was built on a gigantic scale and although deprivations after the Reformation stripped away much of its finery, enough remains to interest even the most casual visitor. It stands in the centre of the east-coast town. One of the remaining towers has a large round window that is fondly called the 'o' in Arbroath.

When William died, he was buried under the high altar, and although nothing of the original tomb remains, a modern plaque marks his last resting place. It stands at the site of the high altar in the old abbey. The abbot's house in the grounds at least still stands complete, and has within it part of an effigy believed to come from William's tomb.

William's queen was Ermengarde, and not to be outdone, she founded her own abbey at Balmerino – which has since been badly stripped of its stonework, though you can still discern much of the original cloisters.

Ermengarde was buried under the high altar at Balmerino, which was admired for its pleasant surroundings. The ruins stand on the south shore of the Firth of Tay, between Newburgh and Newport, a few miles west of the Tay Rail Bridge, on an unclassified road, and the countryside round about has many quiet lanes that are a joy to drive.

While in the vicinity, it is worth visiting the ruins of another ancient abbey – Lindores, just east of Newburgh, which has connections with William Wallace. And in Coupar Angus there are the remains of a Cistercian monastery, founded by Malcolm IV. It is one of the boy king's few tangible achievements.

His great grandparents, Malcolm Canmore and his queen Margaret, later to be canonised and better known to most Scots as St Margaret, left more in the way of memorials – especially the magnificent Dunfermline Abbey.

Entering Dunfermline's Pittencrieff Glen by the gate at the front of the abbey, you come across the remains, to the right of the path, of King Malcolm's Tower. This old tower was built between 1057 and 1070 as a residence for Malcolm Canmore, and crowns a knoll rising 70 feet above the stream through the glen. The name 'Dunfermline' comes from this fort. It means 'the fort by the bend in the water', and the burn in the Pittencrief Glen below does take a bend round this site. Today all that remains is a fragment of the south and west walls, rising to a height of about eight feet.

Malcolm, Margaret and various relics connected with her remained at Dunfermline till the Reformation, when Philip II of Spain had them removed to Madrid. At the end of the 18th century, it was reported that two urns containing the bones of Malcolm and Margaret were kept within the Escorial, a palace in Madrid. It seems that at least some of their remains are still there. It is quite mind-boggling to imagine the remains of an early medieval king and queen of Scotland ending up in Spain.

The beautifully illuminated prayer book of St Margaret was missing for 800 years, and unexpectedly turned up at a book sale in 1857, where it was purchased by the Bodleian Library in Oxford for six pounds. The book is still in its possession. I feel that this artefact, like many others, should be kept within the Kingdom of Scotland, as it is a Scottish item, paid for by the Scottish people. A facsimile of it is kept in St Margaret's Chapel, within Edinburgh Castle.

Many of our important historical assets are scattered among the museums of Europe. Perhaps one day we will see all that is rightfully ours returned.

CHAPTER NINE

Viking defeat at Largs

Revisiting 1263 and all that.

UNLIKE THEIR COUNTERPARTS in England, most of whom are buried within Westminster Abbey, the royals of Scotland since the time of Iona are scattered in graves all over the face of the land.

William the Lion's son, Alexander II, died on the island of Kerrera, near Oban, while preparing to quell unrest in the Hebrides. He took ill aboard his ship, anchored in Horseshoe Bay, and was carried ashore and died at a spot still known as Dalrigh, or 'The King's Field'. Alexander II must have had a liking for Melrose Abbey, for great efforts were made to transport his body right across Scotland to be interred beneath the high altar there.

His son, Alexander III, had a long and prosperous reign. Many coins survive from this period showing that, economically, things were going well in Scotland. More mints for the production of coinage existed in Alexander's time than at any other era in Scotland's history. 18 different mints have been identified from the inscriptions on coins, and these include such diverse sites as Inverness, Renfrew, Berwick, Ayr, Roxburgh, Perth and Montrose.

Alexander III's main claim to fame, however, was his victory at the Battle of Largs in 1263, when he grasped control of the Hebrides from the Norsemen, in what was in reality little more than a major skirmish. Its impact has reverberated down the ages, however, as a significant turning point in Scotland's history. Lest we forget, Edinburgh's National Portrait Gallery has a large painting on a wall at first-floor level, depicting a scene from the historic fight.

The Viking fleet had suffered much damage due to heavy storms before the battle, and that – coupled with some skilful delaying tactics on the part of Alexander III – meant that the

Viking longships were compelled to make a landing at Largs, with only a part of their whole strength.

The battle, resulting in a complete victory for the Scots, effectively put an end to Norse claims of sovereignty over not only the Western Isles of Scotland but much of the coast of the western mainland, where the dragon-prowed longships held sway.

The site of this battle can be visited, and is marked by a large monument known fondly as the Pencil (which does indeed look like a giant upright pencil) at the southern end of Largs, on the seashore, a little north of the modern marina.

There was a mound or tumulus in Largs known locally as either 'Margaret's Law' or 'Hakon's Tomb', which consisted of a large flat stone supported by two others. It was opened in 1780 and found to contain five stone coffins holding skulls and other bones, while many human bones and funeral urns were found above and around the coffins. From this discovery it was immediately concluded that this was the burial place of many of the slain from the battle. But there was no glorious death for our king, Alexander III, the victor of such a heroic episode as the Battle of Largs. A battle that is still mentioned with pride by Scots today.

Like so many Kings of Scots, Alexander met an untimely end. He broke his neck in a fall after his horse stumbled as he rode along the cliffs near Kinghorn, in Fife, on a dark and stormy night.

A monument in the shape of a Celtic cross marks the spot where Alexander's body was found. This stands beside the A92 coast road between Burntisland and Kinghorn, overlooking the sands of Pettycur Bay.

Unlike his father Alexander II, Alexander III did not have to travel too much further after his demise – he was buried in Dunfermline Abbey. But even that assured no peace in the afterlife. His tomb was destroyed by zealots out to smash any trace of idolatry at the Reformation. He would be surprised at how much his death was to change his kingdom. His only heir was his little granddaughter, the Maid of Norway, and she died before she could become queen. There was no direct heir to the throne of Scotland.

Edward Longshanks of England was waiting in the wings and saw his chance. The Wars of Independence were about to begin.

CHAPTER TEN

On Wallace's trail

*Little real trace, but many a place, linked to
the famed freedom fighter.*

WE HAVE ALMOST NOTHING tangible in the way of artefacts from
William Wallace's lifetime. However, there are many places in our
landscape with a Wallace connection. So we can at least say he has
left his impression on the face of the countryside.

There is a debate over where he was born, but a little detective
work shows that really there is no doubt that the place was
Elderslie, in Renfrewshire. There was an archaeological dig here in
late 1998, which revealed the foundations and remains of a fortified building from the 1250s. As Wallace was born in the early
1270s, these could well have been the remains of his birth-house.

There is a beautiful monument at the site, raised in 1910 by
public subscription, and its base contains plaques with scenes from
Wallace's life.

The low walls beside this monument are the remains of later
Wallace properties, built on the site by William's descendants in the
1500s. Unbelievably, these buildings were entire until the 1970s,
when the local council had them demolished. It seems astonishing
that buildings connected to a national hero could be just swept
away like that.

Many folk tales are told of Wallace's exploits as a youth, and
monuments have been erected in various localities in remembrance
of him. Paisley Abbey, where it is believed he received his early
schooling, has a Wallace stained-glass window, and the doorway
from his era still exists in the cloisters.

Ayr has two statues of Wallace. One is on the Wallace Tower,
the other at first-floor level in Newmarket Street, but a rather more
striking memorial is the large cairn erected to the memory of not only

Wallace but also our great national bard, Robert Burns. It stands by the River Ayr in the grounds of Auchencruive agricultural college.

Burns was born at nearby Alloway, and as a boy marvelled at the tales of Wallace's exploits. It was believed Wallace had spent time hiding out in Leglen Wood, the remains of which stand around the cairn, and Burns as a lad explored the area. He stated that he hoped when he was grown, that he would be able to write something dedicated to Wallace that would do justice to the great man. This came to pass, as Burns wrote the stirring words to 'Scots Wha Hae'.

Aberdeen has its magnificent statue too, with Wallace giving 'defiant answer to the English forces at Stirling Bridge'. It stands in Union Terrace Gardens. A little south, outside Stonehaven, stand the grim ruins of Dunnottar Castle. The remains of its 13th century chapel are a reminder of Wallace's raid here. The English garrison made a last stand inside this chapel, but Wallace fired it, burning the occupants within.

Lanark also has a large part to play in the Wallace story. It was here that his sweetheart Marion was slain. A small plaque at the top of the Castlegait marks the site of her family's house.

There is a Wallace statue in Lanark, which, like so many others built in Victorian times, shows Wallace as a middle-aged man, rather than the 20-something he was at the height of his power.

The site of the castle where Wallace exacted his terrible revenge on the English sheriff and garrison for Marion's murder is now the bowling green at Castlebank Park.

Stirling is the scene of his great victory over the occupying forces in 1297. The bridge from Wallace's time was just a few yards upstream of the old footbridge standing today. The battle was fought where the modern Causewayhead Road now runs. The Abbey Craig, where Wallace marshalled his forces, is today topped by the National Wallace Monument, which contains what is believed to be the sword of our hero.

After Stirling Bridge, Wallace invaded northern England, and on his return was created Guardian of Scotland. A plaque marking this event exists in the old Kirk of the Forest, which stands near the town centre in Selkirk.

In 1298, Wallace's great adversary, Edward Longshanks, brought his vast armies north and defeated the Scots with great loss at the Battle of Falkirk. This battle was fought over the Westquarter Burn, most likely in the area around Woodend Farm.

From then on, Wallace resorted to guerrilla warfare. The end came in 1305, when he was captured near Glasgow. The Celtic cross that marks the spot in Robroyston is unknown to most Glaswegians, as is the nearby Wallace Well, where he had his last drink as a free man.

He was taken south to London for his show trial and shameful murder. A plaque on the floor of Westminster Hall shows the place where he learned of his awful fate. He was slaughtered at the butchers' yards of Smithfield. Today a fine granite plaque on the wall of St Bartholomew's Hospital at West Smithfield marks the spot.

CHAPTER ELEVEN

The hero king

Where the spirit of Bruce can still be found.

ROBERT BRUCE IS REGARDED as Scotland's greatest king. He has been denigrated over the years, for not being as single minded as Wallace, for being of Norman stock, but the hard truth remains that Scotland would have ceased to exist in the early 1300s if not for his sterling work.

He was born on 11 July 1274, most likely at Turnberry Castle, the ruins of which can still be seen beside the lighthouse on the famous golf course. His mother was Countess of Carrick and as Turnberry Castle was her house, it seems safe to assume that this is where he was born. He was several generations a Scot on his father's side, and his mother was of the old Celtic stock, so to call him a Norman seems a bit wide of the mark.

In February 1306, he stabbed to death his main rival, Sir John Comyn, in the church attached to Greyfriars monastery, in Dumfries, before assuming the crown. The site of this incident is marked by a plaque in the town centre, just to the west of the Burns statue in the aptly named Burns Square.

Bruce immediately gathered a small army and headed north to be crowned – at the Moot Hill at Scone, which still stands in the grounds of Scone Palace.

He received an early crushing defeat at the Battle of Methven, the site of which lies just east of Methven Castle, near Perth. With a band of followers, he took to the hills to regroup. English troops captured his womenfolk and treated them barbarously, locking them in cages for people to peer at like animals in a zoo. Three of his four brothers suffered bloody executions.

Legend claims that at this low ebb, Bruce was helped by watching a spider try to anchor its web. If the arachnid could win, then so could he. Several caves in Scotland are said to have hosted this event, such as the King's Caves in Arran, or one that sits close to the M74 in Dumfriesshire – signposted from the centre of Kirkpatrick-Fleming.

Bruce's first blow for his land's freedom came at Glen Trool in Galloway in April 1307. A carved boulder marks his victory at the road end above Loch Trool.

He struck north and defeated another English army at Loudoun Hill, an extinct volcano towering above Darvel in Ayrshire. There is a plaque on the summit of Loudoun Hill commemorating this victory. Reaching the top involves a stiff haul, but an easier ascent can be made from the 'back', north of the hill.

Bruce then took to fighting a guerrilla campaign, taking castles by stealth, ousting English garrisons and attacking supply columns. His true genius lay in his manner of warfare. There were 10 Englishmen for every Scot, and Bruce used subterfuge, and the land of Scotland itself, to counteract their numerical superiority.

The crunch came when his last surviving brother, Edward, struck a deal with the governor of Stirling Castle to have it brought under Scots control. The English saw this as a direct call to arms, and marched a mighty army north to crush the Scots once and for all.

The two armies met at Bannockburn in June 1314. This battle was fought on a grand scale, the main fight lasting two days.

The Bannockburn Heritage and Visitor Centre gives an audio-visual account of these events, and stands on the ground where Bruce mustered the Scots army. Two stones in the grounds of Randolphfield police headquarters are said to mark where the Scots held the English charge during the first day's conflict.

The main battle of the second day saw the Scots forcing the English army back against the gorge of the Bannock Burn. Parking in Bannockburn village and walking up into the gorge gives a good idea of what a formidable barrier this must have been to an armoured cavalry host. Bruce's spearmen forced the English back and over the northern lip of the gorge, to plummet into ruin below.

But the victory at Bannockburn was not the end of the war.

Bruce launched raids into England to try to get Scotland's rights to nationhood recognised. He won several battles on English soil that are largely forgotten. The most notable were the Chapter of Myton, fought at the village of Myton north of York; the Battle of Byland, on the Hambleton Hills near Thirsk, where Scots almost captured the King of England; and the clash at Stanhope in which the Scots humbled the English forces entirely.

In 1328, England finally conceded Scotland's right to independent nationhood. Bruce was to die the following year, at Cardross on the River Leven, north of Dumbarton, on 7 June 1329. He was buried in Dunfermline Abbey and his tomb is marked by a brass plaque.

Bruce's heart, after being taken on crusade by the Black Douglas, was buried in Melrose Abbey, where a stone plaque in the grounds marks its resting place.

There are several statues commemorating Bruce scattered across Scotland's landscape, but surely the most beautiful is the one on the field at Bannockburn itself. Pilkington Jackson sculpted it. The face of the statue is recreated from a cast of Bruce's skull.

It is a fitting memorial to the hero king of Scots.

CHAPTER TWELVE

The powers behind Bruce's throne

All the king's top men and what became of them.

AFTER BANNOCKBURN IN 1314, Robert Bruce, King of Scots, became known as the 'First Knight of Christendom' throughout Europe. But, of course, the devastating run of victories against English rule was not just down to Bruce himself – he had some exceptional captains.

There was Keith the Marischal, the captain of cavalry. There was Walter, Bruce's High Steward. Edward, King Robert's brother, was a dashing leader. But shining above even these were James Douglas and Thomas Randolph, two of the finest commanders of men Scotland has ever produced.

After Bannockburn, where both had excelled, they became the scourge of northern England, crossing and recrossing the Border on hit-and-run raids to try to force England to the negotiating table.

At Myton-on-Swale, north-west of York, these two annihilated an English army composed largely of churchmen. Later the Scots would derisively call this episode the Chapter of Myton because of the amount of clergy among the slain. The field where this encounter took place can still be visited. Crossing the old bridge over the River Swale at Myton takes you on to the ground where the English were forced back against the river.

Randolph was one of the commanders of Bruce's army of invasion into Ireland, his level-headedness proving its worth again and again during this campaign.

Bruce joined Randolph and Douglas at the Battle of Byland in 1322, when the Scots fought their way up the steep gradient of Sutton Bank in the Hambleton Hills, on the line of the modern A170 road, smashing their way through the English lines, and almost capturing Edward II of England, who was in residence at Rievaulx Abbey at the time. The imposing ruins of Rievaulx still stand, a little north of the village of Helmsley on the A170.

When Edward III came to the throne of England in 1327, he carried on with the tired old 'Lord Paramount of Scotland' argument, and prepared to renew the war with Scotland. Bruce again sent Douglas and Randolph south. Edward III confronted them at Stanhope on the River Wear in County Durham, and asked them to renege on their strong position on the hillside and come down and fight.

Douglas and Randolph replied: 'We are deep in your country of England. We have burnt and wasted it, and if you do not like it come and dislodge us, because we are very pleased where we are.'

Douglas launched a night raid into the English camp, the Scots stabbing the sleeping English troops with their spears, crying: 'Douglas! Douglas! You shall all die, Lords of England!' Douglas actually reached the English king's tent, but several of Edward's retainers threw themselves on top of him to save his life.

Before the English could retaliate, the Scots slipped away. Edward III wept tears of frustration at his inability to bring Douglas and Randolph to battle. Their attacks were responsible for the English king signing the peace treaty in 1328.

After Bruce's death, Douglas carried his heart on crusade, eventually dying in battle in Teba in Andalusia, Spain, in 1330. He is buried in the Church of St Brides in Douglas, Lanarkshire.

Randolph became the Guardian of Scotland during the minority of Bruce's son, but he did not long outlive Douglas. Randolph died in Musselburgh. The inhabitants stood guard around the house where he lay ill until news of his death was announced and, ever since, Musselburgh has been known as the 'Honest Toon'. He probably died of some illness, but the story was spread around Scotland that an English assassin had poisoned him.

Randolph was buried in Dunfermline Abbey, but unfortunately no trace of his tomb now remains.

CHAPTER THIRTEEN

Where death triumphed

Bruce had gone, but the battles went on.

IT WAS UNFORTUNATE for the Scots that the son of King Robert Bruce, David II, did not take on board the legacy left by his illustrious father. The methods of Bruce were summed up in Good King Robert's Testament, written in the 1300s:

> On foot should be all Scottish war. Let hill and marsh their foes debar. And woods as walls prove such an arm. That enemies do them no harm. In hidden spots keep every store, And burn the plainlands them before. So, when they find the land lie waste, Needs must they pass away in haste; Harried by cunning raids at night. And threatening sounds from every height. Then as they leave with great array, Smite with the sword and chase away. This is the councel and intent, Of Good King Robert's Testament.

These sound principles were ignored to Scotland's cost, at defeats like Dupplin Moor in 1332. The battle site is by the A9, south-west of Perth. Or at Halidon Hill in 1333, just outside Berwick on Tweed. On both these occasions the Scots took on the English in a frontal assault. As the English outnumbered them and had superiority in weaponry, it was foolishness of the highest degree.

Bruce's advice could also have saved the day at the defeat at Neville's Cross, where David II was captured by the English. This battle site is straddled by the A1, just west of Durham.

King David was eventually returned to Scotland, for the ransom of 10,000 marks per annum, but he unexpectedly died at Edinburgh Castle in February 1371. Luckily, ransoms do not have to be paid for dead men, so Scotland could breathe a sigh of relief.

Next up as ruler was Robert II, the first of the Stewart line of kings. Robert II himself would no doubt have been very surprised to know that he was the founder of a dynasty that was to rule for 300 years – and one that was to inherit the throne of England, in the shape of James VI and I. In fact, the Stewart dynasty is the longest running in European history, so it is strange that there is not a wealth of statues to them in our cities. Certainly there are none to any of the Stewart monarchs who ruled before the Act of Union.

The Scots won a major victory during Robert II's reign – at Otterburn in Northumberland in August 1388, the famous battle 'won by a dead man'.

The fighting raged throughout the night on the marshy ground below the Roman wall. As the two sides fell apart to draw breath, James, Earl of Douglas, who was leading the Scots, was mortally wounded.

As he was carried to the rear, Douglas was asked how he felt, and replied: 'Right evil, but thank God few of my fathers died in their beds.'

In the evocative 'Ballad of Otterburn', Douglas said:

'My wound is deep, I am fain to sleep, Take thou the vaward of me; And hide me by the bracken bush that grows on yon lilye-lee'.

He then ordered his lieutenants to take his banner back to the fight, to shout his war cry 'Douglas!' and to let no one know that he was dead.

Towards dawn the exhausted English commander, Henry Percy – better known by his proud nickname 'Hotspur' – was asked by Sir John Montgomery of Eaglesham to yield. He said he would, but to whom?

'Thou shalt not yield to lord nor loon, Nor yet shalt thou to me, But yield thee to the bracken bush, Grows on yon lilye-lee'.

Hotspur yielded and Montgomery was able to extract a huge ransom for his safe return to England. It is said that this ransom money was used to build the mighty Polnoon Castle, the scant ruins of which stand just to the east of the village of Eaglesham today.

The battlesite at Otterburn can be visited. A monument stands a little north of the village of the same name, which is just off the

A68 – the road that runs south after crossing the Border at Carter Bar, south of Jedburgh.

Robert II died within Dundonald Castle. It stands atop its mound above Dundonald village in Ayrshire, a stone monument to the early days of the Stewart reign of power, and is open to the public.

CHAPTER FOURTEEN

Murdoch's last view

Heads had to roll on James I's return.

WHILE JAMES I OF SCOTLAND was a captive in English hands, and the land was under the control of Albany as regent, the Lords of the Isles saw their chance to make inroads into mainland Scotland. They came against the royal forces at Harlaw on the River Urie. Perhaps I should call it Red Harlaw, as this is the name that most of our history books give this bloody encounter, which was a great slaughter but basically settled nothing and ended in stalemate.

The site can be visited a little north of the A96, west of Inverurie, and the battle's monument is a large hexagonal, pointed pillar, with signboards giving the details of the fight.

Another Scots army won a resounding victory fighting against the English at Bauge in France, an almost forgotten battle, probably because victory was achieved on foreign soil. But one or two mementoes of this France-based victory can still be found in Scotland.

Where the River Stinchar flows into the sea at Ballantrae in southern Ayrshire, above the junction of the B7044 and the A77 coast road, stand the ruins of Ardstinchar Castle. This castle was built by one of the Kennedy family. He had fought with great honour at Bauge and was given a gift of money by the grateful French king. This newfound wealth allowed him to build his impressive castle here. It is now in a ruinous state, the main tower looking dangerously close to collapse, but enough survives to give us a little glimpse of what an impressive place it once was.

By the time James was released from his English captivity, his uncle Albany, the regent, was dead, but Albany's son – therefore James's cousin; Murdoch – was regent in his place. Murdoch had let the country go to rack and ruin, and for this James had him executed, along with his two sons, at Stirling.

You can still visit the spot of Murdoch's execution. On top of Gowan Hill – a spur of the castle rock, which juts out in the direction of the old bridge at Stirling – stands the 'Heading Stone', or rather, beheading stone. This stone is now covered with a semi-circular iron grille. Nearby stand two cannon – making a noticeable landmark from the area of Stirling Bridge.

Many figures from history were to meet their end here, with head lain upon the stone, but it must have been even more galling for Murdoch, as from here he could see the countryside that encircled his castle of Doune, only eight miles away to the north west. Doune Castle, a mighty medieval fortress, is open to the public, and stands above the River Teith on the outskirts of Doune itself.

James I of Scotland was to eventually die at the hands of assassins in 1437, at the Dominican Friary in Perth. James was fond of tennis and had a tennis court built at Perth for his pleasure. A similar court can still be seen at Falkland Palace. James was in the habit of losing expensive tennis balls down a hole at the side of the court and so he had one of his masons fill it in. When trying to escape from his assassins, James dropped into a sewer to effect a getaway, but found his exit blocked. He had unwittingly had his escape route filled in by the mason, and he died there, trying to fend off his attackers with his bare hands.

Though the monastery has gone, a plaque in Perth's Blackfriars Street marks the spot. Strangely James was buried in another Perth monastery, the Carthusian, which has also gone. But a pillar inscribed with James' name amongst others of note marks the site of this monastery. It stands at the junction of King Street and County Place in front of the old James VI Hospital. Strangely enough, James's killers were also slain on the Heading Stone at Stirling, after suffering days of torture on the orders of a wrathful Queen Joan, James's widow. Part of that torture entailed her husband's assassins being strapped to a throne with red-hot iron crowns placed on their heads. She was determined to teach a harsh lesson to any who fancied their chances of usurping the throne of Scotland.

CHAPTER FIFTEEN

A king's dark deed

The spot where James II murdered the Earl of Douglas.

JAMES II AND HOLYROOD ABBEY are linked inextricably. In fact, James was born, crowned, married and buried within this old building, which still stands in ruins beside the later Holyrood Palace at the base of Edinburgh's Royal Mile.

Tours of Holyrood end with access to the abbey, so while it is only a shadow of its former magnificence, you can still wander around it and cast your mind back to when it was a royal residence.

James's father died when he was only six, and so his mother took him to the safety of Edinburgh Castle. Due to the unrest following his father's murder at Perth, James was crowned, on 25 March 1437, at Holyrood, so breaking the long tradition that Scots kings should be enthroned at Scone – reckoned in this case to be too close to Perth for safety.

While he was young, powerful lords used James as a pawn, as having custody of the king basically put control of the state into your hands. James was shuttled between Edinburgh and Stirling castles – the former in the control of Crichton, the latter in control of Livingston, two lords eager for power. It must have been strange for James, being shifted back and forth between these two similar buildings.

In the early years of James's reign, many lords took the law into their own hands – such as the powerful Tiger Earl of Crawford. The remains of his castle can still be discerned, among trees on the opposite bank of the Clyde from the village of Crawford, off the M74 in southern Lanarkshire.

Not too far north of here is the Kirk of St Bride in Douglas, the last resting place of James the Gross, the Lord of Douglas at this time. His ornate tomb has survived.

James II was responsible for the murder of William, the eighth Earl of Douglas, in February 1452. The earl was invited to dinner at Stirling Castle, where hot words were exchanged. James leapt forward and plunged his dagger into Douglas's throat. Other lords took their cue from their monarch, and later 26 stab wounds were found on the earl's body – which was thrown from a window to the garden below.

This window was later replaced in stained glass, bearing the Douglas coat of arms, with the three stars on blue, above the blood-red heart of Robert Bruce. It stands at first-floor level above the rear garden.

The skeleton of a partially armed man was found buried in this garden in 1797. It was believed that this might be William Douglas – after all, his death caused so much of a furore that they would not have been able to remove the body from the castle and would have had to bury it in situ. James's reign is peppered with stories of his feud with the Douglas family – and of his interest in artillery.

A story is told that, at the siege of Threave Castle in 1455, a cannonball flew between the Douglas laird and his wife inside, as they sat down to dinner. Threave Castle, a picturesque ruin on an island in the River Dee, three miles west of Castle Douglas, is open to the public.

An exploding cannon at the siege of Roxburgh Castle killed James in 1460. It was ironic that his interest in cannon was to prove his undoing. A thorn tree in the grounds of the later Floors Castle marks the spot.

CHAPTER SIXTEEN

Home of the family who ran Scotland

Dean Castle is still in excellent repair, on the trail of James III.

AFTER HIS FATHER'S DEATH at Roxburgh Castle, the heir to the throne was brought south from Edinburgh to the scene. The new monarch, James III of Scotland, was crowned king at Kelso Abbey, the scant ruins of which are open to the public. They stand in the centre of the town of the same name, overlooking the junction of the rivers Teviot and Tweed.

During James's minority, the Boyd family – huge landowners in the Kilmarnock area – seized the reins of power in Scotland. They more or less ran the country for several years. They had been granted land in Ayrshire after fighting with distinction at the Battle of Largs in the reign of Alexander III, and Robert Bruce ratified these possessions.

For a small entry charge, it is well worth visiting Dean Castle on the northern side of Kilmarnock to see the old home of the Boyd family. There is the original massive old foursquare tower as well as a newer palace block surrounded by curtain walling, all in a beautiful state of repair. The buildings contain some marvellous bits and pieces, especially in the way of ancient arms and armour, and there is a collection of old musical instruments.

A little to the south-east of Dean stands a large, tree-covered mound. This was the site of an earlier timber castle, which fell into disuse when the first part of Dean – the aforementioned foursquare tower – was constructed in stone.

James III's demise came shortly after the Battle of Sauchieburn in 1488. Sauchieburn has no monument marking its site, although it is reckoned the main action took place at a spot called Little Canglar, on the Sauchie Burn about a mile west of the battlefield of Bannockburn.

Another Bannockburn connection is the abiding story that

James III carried the same great two-handed sword at Sauchieburn that Bruce had carried at his nearby victory in 1314. This sword was later kept at Clackmannan Tower, still standing above the town of the same name. The widow of the last laird of Clackmannan, an ardent Jacobite, was visited by Robert Burns, and she was so impressed with the poet that she fetched down Bruce's sword and 'knighted' him in the castle hall. This sword is now in the keeping of the Earl of Elgin.

The presence of Bruce's sword did not stand James in good stead, however, and he fled the battlefield in the direction of the Forth, to try to escape in one of the ships of his admiral, Sir Andrew Wood, who hailed from Largo in Fife. The story runs that James's horse shied when they unexpectedly came across a miller's wife drawing water from the Bannock Burn. She took James indoors but his pursuers found him there and stabbed him to death. Legend states that the miller's name was Beaton, and this Beaton's Mill survived until 1954, when it was accidentally burned down.

Its site – the last vestiges of walls marking the fatal spot – can still be visited. It stands beside the Bannock Burn by a little footbridge at Milton, about a hundred metres downstream from the point where the burn flows under the A872.

James's last resting place is in Cambuskenneth Abbey, the ruins of which stand in a loop of the Forth opposite Stirling. He was buried under the high altar beside his wife, and their tomb was rediscovered in 1864, when a new monument was erected over their remains.

The gate at Cambuskenneth is generally unlocked in daylight hours, so you can visit the tomb of a king and also have a look at the interesting gargoyles that adorn Cambuskenneth's surviving belltower.

CHAPTER SEVENTEEN

Defeat at Flodden

*One of the tragedies of James IV's life was that
he never knew his father.*

JAMES IV WAS TAKEN to the port of Leith with the rest of the victorious army after the Battle of Sauchieburn. When Sir Andrew Wood, Admiral of the Scottish Navy, walked into the room, young James, seeing his noble bearing, asked: 'Sir, are you my father?'

This sad scene shows how much James had been alienated from his family, and the question brought tears to the eyes of the brave Sir Andrew, who already knew James III was dead. But Sir Andrew Wood was to prove a stalwart warrior in the service of James IV, just as he had been to his father.

One of Sir Andrew's great victories took place when three English men-of-war tried to intercept his two ships, the *Flower* and the *Yellow Carvel*, in the Firth of Forth. Henry VII of England feared Sir Andrew so much that he had put £1,000 reward – to be paid annually for life – on Sir Andrew's head. The battle lasted for two arduous days until the English ships finally surrendered in the Tay, off Dundee. Crowds, following along the cliffs of Fife, watched the running sea battle.

James's appetite for naval matters was obviously whetted by such deeds.

At Airth – today, a little upstream from the Kincardine Bridge over the Forth – James developed a royal dockyard, which was watched over by Airth Castle. So that the castle would be kept in good repair for this task, he granted £100 for its partial rebuilding – and although it is now a hotel, this renovated part is still visible.

Airth today is a sleepy little village, standing inland from the river due to modern land reclaiming, and it is strange to equate the place with such a hive of medieval sea-faring manufacture, especially as it now stands so far away from the water.

James was a man of diverse tastes, not only dabbling in advancements in the war machinery, but also in alchemy and related experimental ventures.

A poignant reminder survives today of James's existence as a man with dreams, fears and loves, just like the rest of us. He had fallen in love with the fair Margaret Drummond, daughter of the lord at Drummond Castle, near Crieff. Powerful men in Scotland did not like this relationship and wished to make sure there were no impediments to James's proposed marriage to Margaret Tudor of England. The Scottish Margaret and two of her sisters were poisoned at Drummond Castle in 1502.

They were buried within Dunblane Cathedral, where three bluish marble slabs indicate their last resting place. There have been tales that James and Margaret Drummond had been secretly married, but these would seem to be later inventions. The cathedral dates back to the time of David I of Scotland and is open to the public. It stands in the centre of the town of the same name, above the Allan Water.

James's end came in 1513, at the ill-fated Battle of Flodden, which took place on English soil, just a few miles south of Coldstream, the nearest town on the Scottish side of the border.

It was Scotland's worst defeat in battle. If you stand at the modern monument today, looking up at Branxton Hill where the Scots came over the edge and down to the waiting English bill-hooks and annihilation, you will know that it is a place for some contemplation.

The annual 'Common Ridings' of some Border towns – such as Selkirk and Hawick – have their genesis in the carnage of Flodden and its aftermath. At one such event, I heard this remark as the riders mounted their horses:

'Remember lads, you are Scots and you are Borderers. And ye didna' come fae nothing!'

CHAPTER EIGHTEEN

Aftermath of Flodden

Flodden's impact on the reign of James V is easy to appreciate.
But Scots still have reminders of the pain.

THE EARLY YEARS of the reign of James V were spent dealing with the tragedy of Flodden. A new wall was built to defend Edinburgh – the Flodden Wall. Remnants of it can still be found in the city. One part that is easy to visit is the section in Greyfriars Churchyard, the entrance of which is in Candlemaker Row, just opposite the new Museum of Scotland.

The wall was built to counter the expected heavy English invasion. One invasion force came to a sticky end in 1514 in the little-known fight at the Hornshole, near Hawick. The angry youths of the town, determined to avenge their fathers' deaths, annihilated a body of English here.

> Teribus ye Teriodin;
> Sons of heroes slain at
> Flodden,
> Imitating Border Bowmen,
> Aye defend your rights and
> common.

A pillar bearing the legend '1514, Lest we Forget' marks the spot, and stands two miles north-east of Hawick, just off the A698. The Horse Monument in Hawick town centre is also a commemoration of this battle, and the famous Hawick Common Riding is based on it, too.

During James's time, cross-Border reiving was at its height, so much so that the area around Liddesdale was known as the Debatable Land – a reference to the fact that no one seemed to be sure where Scotland ended and England began.

James led an excursion into the Borders in 1530 in an attempt to rectify the situation. He had the Border reivers' leader, Johnie Armstrong, and twenty-four of his followers hanged from trees at Caerlenrig churchyard – the story has become one of our best-known Borders ballads. It is said they raided only English territory, and that James made a huge mistake in executing them. A memorial to Johnie Armstrong still stands in the churchyard at Caerlenrig, near the A7, between Hawick and Langholm, by Teviothead.

The Armstrongs held sway all over this area, and have their own little museum in the village of Newcastleton. This museum even has a sample of moon rock! The Scots invented everything; even the first moonwalk was taken by Neil Armstrong – a descendant of the Border clan.

James V also cemented the Auld Alliance with France, by twice marrying Frenchwomen. He married his first wife, Princess Madeleine of France, at a ceremony in the Cathedral of Notre Dame in Paris in 1537, but she died within two months of her arrival in Scotland.

His second wife, Mary of Guise, had a huge influence here. Many of our fortified tower houses have features – little cap-houses, for example – that look like bits of architecture from French chateaux. This began with Mary of Guise's arrival.

James V was not a popular king. He was half-Tudor; a family for whom the Scots held no love. And there was a streak in his personality that neither the nobility nor the common people could like.

It was this facet of his personality that caused a Scottish army to make only a half-hearted attempt at the Battle of Solway Moss in 1542. The battle site lies some three miles north-east of Gretna, near the A6071. James died shortly after the battle in his palace at Falkland. It is easy to imagine him as an old man, but he was worn out at just 30.

Falkland today is an absolute must for anyone with a penchant for revisiting history. Both the palace and the little town clustered around it are throwbacks to earlier times. Weathered but eternally handsome, Falkland Palace stands under the northernmost flanks of the Lomond Hills in Fife.

CHAPTER NINETEEN

The turmoil of reform

Perth was the centre of the big change that still works on our society today.

RELIGIOUS DIVIDE IN SCOTLAND has always been a catalyst for more than debate. Cunning and guile come to the fore, usually resulting in bloodshed, when matters of faith are at stake. Even our football teams suffer from the blight of sectarianism. I realised at a young age that the west of Scotland must be the only place in the world where, when kids are asked what is the opposite of blue, they reply 'green'.

The early days of change from Roman Catholicism to Protestantism in Scotland were not as clean-cut as they at first appear. Though many in the Catholic Church hierarchy were considered corrupt, Protestantism was seen as playing into the hands of England. The Auld Alliance with France, Scotland's staunchly Catholic ally, was a complicating factor in what was a cause for much deliberation.

St Andrews was the site of much of the early upheaval – an obvious location, as it was always an ecclesiastical centre. One of the earliest martyrs of the Reformation was George Wishart. He was burned at the stake outside the castle of St Andrews, and a cobbled inlay – of the initials 'GW' – marks the spot in the street. Cardinal Beaton, of St Andrews, who ordered this execution, was himself assailed and murdered within the castle, and his body hung from a window. A French force blasted its way into the castle and removed the Protestants from within. They were sent to the galleys to be chained to the oars. One of them was John Knox. He spent some time as a galley slave before returning to Scotland to preach the reformed religion.

St Andrews Castle is open to the public, and although much of it is in ruins, the bottle dungeon in the Sea Tower, all 24 ft of it, and the mine, a siege tunnel dug in 1546, should not be missed. A monument to some of the early religious martyrs burned at St Andrews stands near the Royal and Ancient Golf Club. John Knox's first public sermon was delivered in St Andrews in 1547, in the Holy Trinity Church in South Street.

The one huge drawback of the Reformation was the destruction caused by mobs that were determined to smash anything that smacked of 'Papistry'. This unfortunately included ornate decoration within our churches, including statues, paintings or even tombs. Incredibly, the tomb of Robert Bruce in Dunfermline Abbey was destroyed. A huge loss – though the body was found when the abbey was rebuilt in the early 1800s, and it was replaced under a fine, ornate plaque just inside the abbey entrance.

The first church to undergo the destruction of the Reformation was St John's in Perth. This was one of the greatest and oldest religious buildings in Scotland. So much so that the town was originally called St John's Town of Perth; this name survives in the name of the local football team, St Johnstone.

In 1559, John Knox gave a sermon at St John's, declaring that idolatry was 'odious to God's presence'. The following day, 11 May, when a priest opened the tabernacle on the altar, a young boy threw a stone at him. It missed the priest, but smashed the tabernacle. This deed acted as a signal to the congregation and they began to smash all the ornamentation in the building. News of this spread, and soon the same destruction was taking place at Scone, St Andrews, Stirling, Linlithgow, and at churches in Edinburgh, including Holyrood.

St John's Church is open to the public and stands in the heart of modern Perth, west of St John's Street. The modern interior is relatively austere compared to pre-Reformation days.

As it stands today, the church is of various dates of construction, but the square central tower is the oldest part. It contains several bells, the oldest being the St John the Baptist Bell, dated 1400. Mentions of this church go as far back as our earliest records, some accounts ascribing it to Pictish times.

A visit here takes you back through every era of written Scottish history.

CHAPTER TWENTY

Evidence of Mary's presence

*The Queen of Scots left one of her many marks in Glasgow, and
few folk know about it.*

SCOTLAND ABOUNDS WITH PLACES that have a Mary Queen of
Scots connection. If you get the chance, go and visit a few of them
and cast your mind back to the times when Scotland's one and only
queen regnant (rather than queen consort) was in power.

After the Battle of Pinkie in 1547, Mary, a child of only five,
was taken to an island on the Lake of Menteith to protect her from
England's 'Rough Wooing'. Inchmahome has a ruined priory, and
Mary's little garden, 'Queen Mary's Bower', has survived. A boat
takes you across the water from Port of Menteith, near Aberfoyle,
and the surrounding scenery makes this a special day out.

Jedburgh in the Borders still has an old tower house known as
Queen Mary's House, which is open today as a museum. It was
here that she lay ill after her 60-mile ride over the Border hills to
visit Bothwell at Hermitage Castle. During this journey she fell
from her horse, losing her watch in a bog in the process. Centuries
later, it was found and then kept on display in Jedburgh – but later,
unfortunately, it was stolen. Queen Mary's House stands in a park
between Queen Street and the Jed Water.

Glasgow's south side has its large memorial to the Battle of
Langside (1568) in the area of the city known as Battlefield, just
behind the Victoria Infirmary. But there is another memorial to Mary
only a mile or so away which is unknown to most Glaswegians,
never mind the rest of Scotland.

On the highest point of a small park in Old Castle Road in
Cathcart, stands a stone carved with Mary's initials, marking the
spot where she watched the Battle of Langside.

On the opposite side of the road stands the scant ruin of

Cathcart Castle, visited by Mary. Glasgow City Council demolished this edifice in 1980 on the pretext that it was dangerous. I remember it being complete to the wall head, and I'm sure many individuals would have loved a chance to restore the place – never mind developers – and it was a shame it was pulled down. An act of vandalism. All that survive are fragments of low walling.

In the city's Queen's Park, named after Mary, there stands a boating pond over by Pollokshaws Road. This was originally a bog. It made sense, when the park was being laid out, to turn it into a pond. When the workmen began to dig they uncovered armour and skeletal remains, obviously from the dead of the Battle of Langside. When the fight was over, orders would have been given for the dead to be buried, and the burial party must have made life easier for themselves by using the nearby bog. It made more sense than trying to dig through hard soil.

Mary's great adversary, John Knox, has a statue atop a large pillar in Glasgow's Necropolis. As you climb to the top floor of the nearby Museum of Religion, the statue can be seen to spectacular effect through the large glass panel at the top of the stairs – a clever touch on the part of the architects of this traditionally designed building.

The tomb of Mary Queen of Scots can be visited at Westminster Abbey in London. She had first been buried at Peterborough Cathedral after her murder by the English at Fotheringhay Castle, but when her son, James VI, inherited the throne of England, he had her body exhumed and taken to London. The vault containing her body was opened in 1867. Her coffin was surrounded by many others, mostly later royal children who had died in infancy, including the 18 stillborn babies of Queen Anne. The tomb is surmounted by a white marble likeness of Mary.

CHAPTER TWENTY-ONE

Peace and prosperity under James VI

His people called him many names, including 'Son of Riccio'. But James VI did deserve the name of peacemaker.

THE LITTLE ROOM IN Edinburgh Castle where Mary Queen of Scots gave birth to the future James VI – with some difficulty – can still be visited today. Its small window stands high above Johnstone Terrace.

Apocryphal stories abound of the skeleton of a new-born child being found behind the room's wooden panelling, casting doubts on the legitimacy of James VI as king. Certainly at one point in James's career, the people of Perth jeered him, naming him 'Son of Signeur Davie', as they believed his mother Mary's Italian secretary, Riccio, was his father.

James was crowned at the age of 13 months in the Church of the Holy Rude at Stirling. This church stands at the 'top' of the town, near the castle. His mother had been crowned here 24 years before. The tower also has many bullet marks from a siege in 1651.

James was a strange character, by all accounts. He is variously described as being young and old at the same time, or as 'the wisest fool in Christendom'. He shambled like a halfwit, yet had an education of great depth, courtesy of the brilliant but demanding scholar, George Buchanan. One small mistake and Buchanan would thrash the young James. In the middle of one of these beatings, a lady entered the room and berated Buchanan for handing out such heavy punishment on his monarch. Buchanan replied: 'I have whipped his arse, madam. You may kiss it if you wish!'

For all his learning, James was highly superstitious, witchcraft being one of his peculiar horrors. A story was brought to him of the actions of witches at a church in North Berwick, and an infamous witch trial ensued. The story goes that 94 witches and six wizards conjured up Satan himself, whereupon they opened up the graves and shared out among themselves the fingers and toes of the incumbents. The scant remains of this church still stand in North Berwick, by the harbour. It once stood on an islet joined to the shore by arches, but the land has been reclaimed.

James is an odd individual to be responsible for the Bible as we know it today. He translated it from the original manuscripts, and that's why, on opening almost any Bible today, you will see it states 'King James Version' on the flyleaf.

After all is said and done, however, Scotland went through a period of peace during James VI's reign that it had never seen before. He had a horror of bloodshed, and in most difficult political situations he would try to take the middle ground. Trade thrived under James's kingship, and we can only speculate on the advancement that would have been possible if he had not been keeping a constant eye on the south, waiting for the death of Queen Elizabeth of England and his right of succession towards her throne.

The very last act James performed as King of Scots was to command that a bridge be built, and that bridge stands to this day. As he crossed the River Tweed at Berwick on his journey south, the King found the then bridge to be a 'shoogly' old structure, and this terrified him so much that he immediately instructed the powers-that-be that a new stone bridge must be built in its place.

It stands on 15 arches and is 1,164ft in length. Perhaps it is fitting that the monarch who ruled over two kingdoms should also have united them by a stone bridge in the passing.

CHAPTER TWENTY-TWO

Where our history hangs in the air

The past is ever-present in the fabulous buildings
of antiquity in and around the capital.

ROSSLYN CHAPEL STANDS in the village of Roslin, and is signposted from the village's main thoroughfare. Rosslyn itself is only a few minutes' drive south from the Edinburgh city bypass.

The ornamentation inside the chapel is staggering and although it is today covered in a wash of what looks like white plaster, originally it would have been painted in vivid colours. A carved face within is said to be a copy of the death mask of King Robert Bruce. This is possible, as the face shows the same wounding as is apparent on the cast of Bruce's skull, which was made after the opening of his tomb in Dunfermline in 1819.

Rosslyn is currently very much in vogue as several recent books have made a point of featuring legends surrounding the building, but I have to say some of the claims are fabulous indeed, and many facts seem to have been bent to fit the theory. This should not detract from the jewel that the chapel undoubtedly is, and there is much here to impress the visitor.

If you do visit Rosslyn Chapel, don't miss the nearby Rosslyn Castle, which stands in a stupendous setting, high above Rosslyn Glen. From the chapel, go down the path to the graveyard, and then turn sharp left, following the track. Within the ruins of the medieval castle a later building stands, which is today a private house – so privacy should be respected – but you can walk on to the old drawbridge with its low walls and look over at the long drop on either side.

At sites like this I marvel at the tenacity of the original builders – how long did it take to get those huge stone blocks into place in such a perilous position? One mistake would have had them plummeting to certain death. Perhaps there was a medieval version of Health and Safety at Work that insisted on stringent regulations!

Just before the drawbridge section, a path leads down to the right towards the floor of the glen, where you can admire the castle from below, and see the chapel sitting higher up the hillside. You realise how impregnable such a site must have been in the days before artillery.

A battle was fought against the English invaders in this vicinity in Wallace's time, in which three separate enemy forces were defeated in one day. There is a monument to this battle beside the grounds of the Roslin Institute.

Turning to the Covenant, one of the main sites connected with its turbulent times stands in the heart of our capital city – St Giles Cathedral, on your right as you walk down the Royal Mile from Edinburgh Castle. It was here in St Giles that Jenny Geddes was said to have shouted: 'Ye'll no' read the mass in my lug!' – and threw her stool at Dean Hannay as he read from the service book. Popular myth has it that this helped spark the events leading to the Covenant being drawn up.

St Giles is open to the public, and it has on display one of the copies of the original Covenant. It is a fabulous place to visit, and has that certain aura of peace that only establishments of great antiquity can evoke. It is as if the air is heavy with the presence of the historical events that have taken place within its walls. A church has stood on the site of St Giles since 854.

The cathedral is open to the public at most times, and for a while you can escape the city's bustle and bask in some of its ancient glories. The Thistle Chapel in particular has some fine woodcarving that should not be missed.

CHAPTER TWENTY-THREE

Mortal enemies face eternity together

Not even Montrose could avoid the final defeat and a final irony.

THE MARQUIS OF MONTROSE is remembered for the 'Year of the Battles' when, under his strong leadership, his ill-equipped and usually outnumbered men always seemed incapable of anything but complete victory.

The first of the fights was at Tibbermore – sometimes referred to as Tippermuir – where Montrose's army was outnumbered more than two to one. Most of his men had no better weapons than stones to throw, but they charged and broke their enemy's lines, and the slaughter continued to the streets of Perth itself. The battle site is close to the busy A9, near the Broxden roundabout south-west of Perth, where the A9 and M90 meet. The field of the main conflict is by the row of pylons north of Lamberkine Farm.

Perhaps Montrose's most famous victory was at the Battle of Inverlochy. This battle is remembered not just for the fight itself but also for the astonishing march that took place before it. Montrose's army was far up the Great Glen when word was brought that an army under the Campbell Duke of Argyll was on his tail. Montrose turned his men into the hills amid hideous winter conditions. They crossed the grain of the land to come down on Argyll's position. Argyll's army was caught completely by surprise and a great slaughter took place.

The battle was fought a little north of Fort William, before the ruins of Inverlochy Castle. The Comyn family built this old castle, which stands between the A82 and the River Lochy, in the 1200s. Its many illustrious visitors have included Robert the Bruce. There is a modern hotel nearby that also bears the name 'Inverlochy Castle', so make sure, if visiting, that you have chosen the right building!

The beginning of the end for Montrose came with his capture at Ardvreck Castle. The ruins of Ardvreck stand just north of Inchnadamff, between the A837 and Loch Assynt, and are familiar to drivers heading for the far north of Scotland.

Montrose was executed on the Royal Mile in Edinburgh, beside where the Mercat Cross stands today. Argyll was one of those who called for his execution. His body was cut to pieces for display in various Scottish cities, but in later years as much as possible was gathered and he was buried with ceremony in Edinburgh's St Giles Cathedral in 1661. His remains lie in a small vault reached by a staircase under the Chepman Aisle, on the church's south side, beside the organ. Above stands a memorial erected by his descendants in 1888, which is probably the finest effigy and monument ever erected in Scotland. The craftsmanship is quite exquisite. Probably very few visitors to Edinburgh know of its existence, but it is well worth viewing.

Montrose's great enemy, Argyll, is also buried in St Giles. His ornate tomb stands at the opposite, or north, side of the church, against the Royal Mile. It is ironic that two men who were poles apart should face eternity within the same building.

CHAPTER TWENTY-FOUR

Dunbar: 2 lessons in defeat

*The Scots who gave the 1650 battle to Cromwell
forgot the lesson of 1296*

READING THROUGH THE ACCOUNTS of battles fought by Scots can be depressing. Scots seem to have a mental block when it comes to learning from experience, and on the field of battle they have sometimes made the same mistakes as their forefathers did in earlier engagements.

Robert Bruce, a genius in strategy who could use the terrain itself to help counteract enemy superiority, tried hard to instill basic rules in the Scots to help them in warfare; but the lessons he taught seem to have been quickly forgotten. The fighting capabilities of Scots have never been in doubt. It's just a pity that leadership has too seldom been of the same quality.

One of the most astonishing of the Scots' military defeats must have been the Battle of Dunbar, fought in 1650. The Scots had fought a battle there in 1296 – the opening battle of the Wars of Independence. The English army had occupied Dunbar and its castle, and the Scots army appeared on the height of Doon Hill, behind the town. As the English army deployed, the Scots came down from their unassailable position, believing the English were breaking up in disorder – when they arrived, they discovered that the English were ranked in good battle order, and the Scots were easily routed. This ended with King John Balliol being exiled to France.

So 354 years later, Cromwell's army occupied Dunbar and its castle. The Scots again held the height of Doon Hill behind the town. They had a vast superiority in numbers – 23,000 men to Cromwell's 11,000. They were unassailable on their hilltop and had Cromwell in a trap, but they again came down off the hill to meet Cromwell's army ranked in good battle order and, again, were annihilated. 4,000 were slain and 10,000 taken prisoner. It seems incredible that not only had the same mistake been made twice, but it had been made twice in the same location.

The site of the earlier, 1296 defeat is east of Dunbar, just before the village of Spott. The 1650 Cromwellian defeat was slightly further east, the main action having taken place where the A1087 meets the A1 at Broxburn, east of Dunbar.

The original position of the Scots, Doon Hill, towers over all, and the topography of the ground has changed very little, so it is possible to imagine both battles on their respective days. Both are marked on the Ordnance Survey Landranger Map, sheet 67.

A monument to the 1650 battle was raised in 1950, a roughly carved stone which bears some words of Carlyle: 'Here took place the brunt or essential agony of the Battle of Dunbar'. It stands in Broxburn, a little north of the A1.

If visiting Dunbar, the town standing some 28 miles east of Edinburgh, take a look at the old townhouse with its six-sided tower in the High Street. The Mercat Cross stands nearby. The townhouse was built in 1620, so it would have been familiar to those involved in the battle in 1650.

Dunbar's ruined castle sits on a rock above the harbour. There has been a castle here since the first recordings of Scottish history, but it has deteriorated even since my first visit. It was originally built on several different rocks, each connected by covered walkways. One of these walkways or stone bridges still stood about 10 years ago, but has since collapsed into the sea.

There was a famous siege here in 1339, when 'Black Agnes', daughter of Thomas Randolph, a hero of Bannockburn, brilliantly defended the castle. As the English missiles crashed against the stonework, Black Agnes casually brushed her handkerchief against the ramparts, as if scorning the damage caused by the English artillery.

CHAPTER TWENTY-FIVE

Cromwell's death and dishonouring

Thanks to Cromwell, we are less of a nation.

LIKE SO MANY ENGLISHMEN before him, Oliver Cromwell was determined to subjugate the Kingdom of Scotland. To effect this, he built five great fortresses at Leith, Perth, Ayr, Inverlochy and Inverness. These edifices cost the best part of £100,000 each to construct – a vast sum in those days; the equivalent of many tens of millions in this day and age.

The fort at Inverlochy formed the basis of the later Fort William, the name eventually being transferred to the nearby town. One or two wee vestiges have survived of the fort here, a few fragments of walling at the loch side, and the original old archway in the town's graveyard. But the bulk of the fort was swept away to make room for the town's railway station.

There is a remnant of the Ayr fortifications visible just in front of the Citadel Leisure Centre on the south side of the mouth of the River Ayr. This comprises a stretch of walling and a little corner turret. The fort at Ayr incorporated the earlier medieval castle and the tower of St John the Baptist Church. This tower still stands in parkland at Seabank Road, between the town centre and the shore.

Probably the biggest disservice Cromwell did to Scotland was his acquisition of all the records and documentation he could lay his hands on. In his role as Lord Protector, he had this lot taken to London, from whence it would never return. And much of it was put aboard a ship that sank. This was a huge loss, as it left many gaps in our nation's history; accounts of various circumstances and times, lost forever.

After all, what is a nation? What makes me a Scot like any

other? It is a shared heritage, the fact that we have in common the same past and experiences. If that past is partially destroyed, it causes a weakening of what we are. This is why loss of our archives is devastating.

Although the following information has little in the way of a Scottish connection, the fact remains that, for almost a decade, Cromwell ruled Scotland, and in that sense he is important to Scotland's story.

After his death, Cromwell's body was embalmed and buried in Westminster Abbey. A plaque in the Henry vii chapel says it is 'The burial place of Oliver Cromwell 1658–1661'. But the tomb has gone, because after Charles ii's restoration it was decided to dishonour Cromwell as much as possible. His body was exhumed and dragged in its shroud through London from Holborn to Tyburn, long a place of execution, sited at what is now Marble Arch.

Cromwell's corpse was hung there, and then beheaded. The body was buried under the gallows. The exact spot is now the junction of Connaught Place and Connaught Square. Cromwell's head was displayed on Westminster Hall.

During James vii's reign, the head was blown down in a storm and taken home by a guard, who then sold it on as a curiosity. It changed hands a few times for ever-increasing sums of money, and was eventually given to Cromwell's old college at Cambridge. Incredibly, it was 1960 before Cromwell's embalmed head, still in a recognisable state, with the hair of the skimpy beard and moustache still visible, found its last resting place. It was buried in the chapel of Sydney Sussex College, Cambridge.

The exact spot of the burial is a secret, but a plaque at the chapel door reads: 'Near to this place was buried on 25 March 1960 the head of Oliver Cromwell, Lord Protector of the Commonwealth of England, Scotland and Ireland, Fellow Commoner of this College 1616–17'.

CHAPTER TWENTY-SIX

Doomed Argyll's Stone of Destiny

*The exiled earl came home to mount a revolt, but it came to a
head when the Maiden claimed his.*

JAMES VII OF SCOTLAND and II of England reigned for only three
years – 1685 to 1688. When his kingship was announced from the
Cross at Edinburgh on 10 February, it did not in itself cause much
controversy one way or the other. Most Scots had been shocked at
the beheading of his father, Charles I, many years earlier and
although James was a Catholic, he was also a Stewart – the ancient
royal house of Scotland.

The full-scale revolt caused by his policies had still to raise its head.

The Earl of Argyll, however, took great exception to Scotland
being governed by a Catholic, and he returned from exile in
Holland to begin an armed protest. This was the same Argyll who
had been the enemy of Montrose, and who had been instrumental
in securing Montrose's execution in Edinburgh several years before.

Argyll landed in his own clanlands and managed to raise a force
of some 2,500 men. They marched south and took up quarters in
Glasgow, expecting to be backed up by many Scots Protestants.
But the backing did not materialise. Argyll had made too many
enemies with his various machinations, and he found that the
forces arrayed against him were too powerful to overcome. He
ordered his men to retreat to the north-west, but after his army
crossed the Leven north of Dumbarton, incompetent guides led
them into a bog, and to a man the whole army decided to desert,
abandoning all their baggage.

Argyll, meanwhile, had disguised himself as a countryman and
had taken a route along the south side of the Clyde, in the hope of
being ferried across to safety on the north side once he had made
sufficient progress westwards. He had passed Renfrew and was

fording the River Cart when he was recognised by two militiamen. He crossed the river and managed to hold off his pursuers with the aid of his pistols, but assistance came to the militiamen, and one of the pursuers wounded Argyll with a musket shot. When they caught up with Argyll, he was resting against a large boulder and was easily captured.

It seems this boulder still stands, although it has probably been moved slightly from its original position. It is said that the reddish patches seen on it are stains caused by the blood dripping from Argyll's wound. Taking the A8 from Renfrew towards Inchinnan, the road crosses the White Cart and Black Cart in quick succession, and then there is a large lay-by on the right. The stone stands in a corner at the far end of this lay-by, which is immediately adjacent to the end of the runway of Glasgow Airport, and is therefore often busy with plane-spotters who are probably oblivious to the little piece of history right next to them. In fact, in recent years someone has carved the outline of a skull on the boulder – not in any recognition of Argyll, though; this is purely an act of graffiti. Visitors to this spot may also be intrigued to know that Somerled, the first Lord of the Isles, was stabbed to death in this vicinity in the 12th century. His body was taken to Saddell in Kintyre for burial.

Now here is a strange twist: on the Renfrew side of the two River Carts, in the grounds of the Normandy Hotel, there is a stone signposted as the one on which Argyll leaned while wounded. The account of his capture says he had crossed the river, so this is a bit of a mystery. One of these stones is probably the right one. But which? Is it possible that the account stating that he crossed the river is wrong? Has the right stone been brought across the river?

Argyll met his fate on the 'Maiden', the Scots version of the guillotine, which was often used for executions in Edinburgh. The Maiden still survives intact, and can be seen in all its grisly glory in the Museum of Scotland in Chambers Street, Edinburgh.

As Argyll put his head on the block, he is reported to have said, 'Tis the sweetest maiden I ever kissed'. before giving the signal to his executioners that he was ready. He waved his own arm as the signal for the blade to drop. His head was severed instantly.

Argyll lies within St Giles Cathedral on Edinburgh's Royal Mile, his tomb standing against the wall of the north side of the building.

CHAPTER TWENTY-SEVEN

Mountains that saw slaughter

*Even after the awful massacre of Glencoe, the local branch of
Clan MacDonald stayed on in its wild homeland.*

GLEN COE IS PROBABLY the most famous glen in Scotland, not only
because of the massacre, but also because of its popularity as a mountain playground. Like so many others, I have had memorable days
scrambling its peaks and ridges. Most would probably be surprised
to learn that a motor road did not approach from the south until
the 1930s, finally superseding the old military road.

Crossing Rannoch Moor and passing the Kingshouse, Scotland's
oldest inn, most people look at the Rannoch Wall of mighty
Buachaille Etive Mor and assume it is the gateway into Glen Coe.
But for our ancestors, Glen Coe did not really start until you had
passed the famous waterfall at the Study a few miles further west,
and started to descend into the base of the glen. The name 'Etive'
in Buachaille Etive Mor, and its near neighbour Buachaille Etive
Beag, confirms this. The original inhabitants thought of these two
mountains as belonging to Glen Etive, on their eastern side.

Although in this part of Glen Coe the base is quite bare of trees,
there is no monotony, as your eyes are constantly drawn to the
mountain-tops over 3,000 feet above. Bidean nam Bian, the highest
mountain in Argyll, and its projecting spurs, affectionately known
as the Three Sisters, dominate the southern side of the glen. The
northern side is enclosed by the Aonach Eagach (the Notched
Ridge), a three-mile-long wall whose top gives a great scramble.

The glen was originally dotted with a dozen or so villages, and
the massacre was begun through pre-arranged stealth. It had to be,
to ensure that all the scattered populace was surprised.

There is a famous 'Signal Rock' in the glen, and it is a popular
misconception that some sort of signal was given at this spot to

begin the slaughter. But the MacDonalds of Glencoe – or, more specifically, the sept was called MacIain after its chief – inhabited several miles of the glen and giving any signal from one particular point would have been impossible for the murderous Campbells.

This Signal Rock was actually the old clan gathering place, used in emergencies and times of trouble. It stands a little up the glen from the modern information centre, which has been built to deal with more and more visitors. Nearby stands the Clachaig, an old inn, much favoured by climbers. This establishment still bears a sign on its door stating 'No Hawkers or Campbells'.

At the mouth of the glen stands the old village of Carnoch, though everyone today seems to refer to it as Glencoe or Glencoe Village. At the old bridge here over the River Coe, a side road runs a hundred metres or so to a hillock on which stands a slender cross bearing the legend: 'In memory of MacIain, Chief of Glencoe, who fell with his people in the massacre of Glen Coe'.

MacIain was buried on Eilean Munde. This ancient burial isle sits in Loch Leven, just opposite the mouth of the glen. Gravestones can be seen dotted upon it. Many clans used such islands as burial places, perhaps as a throwback to the times when wolves and such-like wandered these hills, and bodies had to be protected from being dug up. Or perhaps this island had a religious connection, many of the early saints having been based on islands.

Many massacres have occurred in Scotland, some far more serious – in numbers at least – than the one that took place here. But I think the reason Glencoe has remained in the forefront of our consciousness is summed up succinctly in the words of W. H. Murray:

> The three points that have appalled the people of our country for 300 years are the cold-blooded planning of mass murder as a matter of public policy by men of responsible position in government; their treacherous abuse of the victims' hospitality as a deliberated chosen means; and the approval of all this by the King, even though not a man of our race.

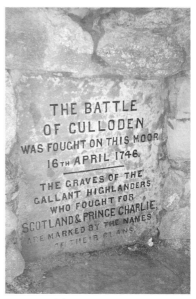

Memorial Cairn, Culloden Battlefield 1746.

Detail from Memorial Cairn, Culloden.

Sword pointing to Flodden Battlefield 1513, Coldstream.

The tomb of Sir James Douglas, St Bride's, Douglas.

The Scottish Parliament, Edinburgh.

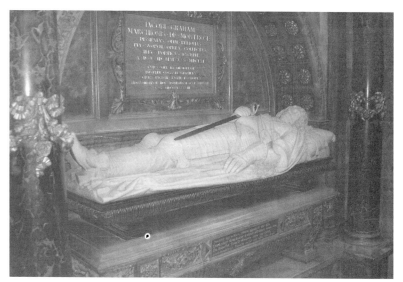

Montrose's Tomb, St Giles Church, Edinburgh.

The Maiden, the
Scottish guillotine,
Museum of Scotland,
Edinburgh.

Mons Meg, Edinburgh Castle.

Edinburgh Castle.

Hunter Brothers' Memorial, East Kilbride.

The King's Knot, Stirling, a possible candidate for Arthur's Round Table.

Stirling Bridge, site of the 1297 battle.

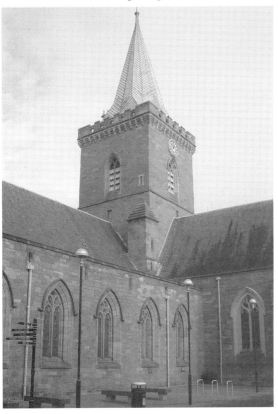

St John's Church,
Perth.

The Round Tower, Brechin.

Monument to the Battle of Sherriffmuir 1715.

Remains of the Roman Antonine Wall near Bonnybridge.

A lock on the Forth and Clyde canal.

Monument in
Glencoe village
to the massacre.

Even the massacre did not sweep the MacIains from this area. They fought bravely at the Jacobite risings of 1715 and 1745. It was the evictions and the introduction of sheep that eventually broke the back of their kinship, and now their descendants are scattered over the face of the planet.

CHAPTER TWENTY-EIGHT

Darien, a feasible scheme

That Darien could have worked for the Scots
is proven by today's Panama Canal.

I REMEMBER BEING TAUGHT at school the details of the 'Darien Scheme' or, as it is sometimes known, the 'Darien Disaster'. The ins and outs upset me then, and the more I have discovered over the years, the more upset I have become.

It was a brilliant idea, and it is no wonder so much of the nation's money was sunk into such a project. After all, the Scots' idea eventually came to fruition in the shape of the Panama Canal. Honest, we could have been contenders! We have produced so many great engineers since, that building a canal across the Isthmus of Panama must have been feasible even for early settlers.

One wee fact that has always intrigued me, strange though it seems, is that the Pacific end of the canal is actually further east than the Atlantic end. This is due to the twists and turns of the isthmus itself.

What is not commonly known is that many Scots had settled in the Gulf of Mexico before Darien. There was a large colony on Barbados, for instance. In fact, Paterson, the mind behind the scheme, had spent some time in the Bahamas. He was well travelled for a Dumfriesshire boy.

It is always possible in museums to recognise coinage issued by the 'Company of Scotland Trading to Africa and the Indies', as the company set up to colonise Darien was known, because they have a wee rising sun at the base of each one. I've noticed several on my travels.

The ships that set out for Darien left from the port of Leith. We can imagine the populace gathered on the quayside to watch them depart on their great adventure. Three of the ships were fitted out as men-of-war. They were the *Caledonia*, the *St Andrew* and the *Unicorn*. Two tenders, laden with provisions, joined these.

William of Orange, or William II of Scotland and III of England as he was by that time, held no love for Scotland. He saw Darien as a slight against the business of the Dutch East India Company, in which, being a Dutchman, he had a vested interest, and against the trading power of England, and made sure many obstacles were laid in the settlers' way. He was in title, King of Great Britain, but he was only interested in ruining whatever advances the people of Scotland tried to make for themselves. William made it known that the 'British' crown would not frown upon any attacks on the Scots.

When the Spanish mounted an attack on the Scots' settlement, one of the Scots, Captain Campbell, assailed them with 200 Highlanders. Though 1,600 strong, the Spaniards were routed with much slaughter.

When news of the failure of Darien reached Edinburgh, there was uproar. But the mob got excited at the news of Campbell's slaughter of the Spaniards. The popular cry went up that all the houses should be illuminated in recognition of this deed, so proud was the populace of this display of 'the auld Scots spirit'.

The mob then marched through the city looking for windows that were unlit, and whenever one was discovered it was smashed – they managed to cause £5,000 worth of damage! Politicians were threatened and, not surprisingly, demands were heard that the Scots crown should be withdrawn from William.

In return, the authorities decided the Edinburgh hangman should be flogged for not punishing the rioters. The executioner of Haddington was hired to inflict the punishment, but refused to flog his brother hangman from the capital. The magistrates of Haddington, scared of losing face, then had their own hangman flogged. This innocent man therefore took all the punishment for an Edinburgh riot that could have led to a civil war and the ousting of William II.

There are still place names in Panama that are a throwback to the Darien Scheme – Punta Escoces, Caledonia Bay and the Caledonian Mountains.

I am reliably assured that there are still remains of the Scots settlement, although it is difficult to locate with the growth of jungle flora now covering it. I'll just have to take someone else's word for that though, as I haven't managed to get my motorcycle that far yet!

CHAPTER TWENTY-NINE

How the Union cost us a mint

Not all the promises made in the articles of Union were kept.

THE GREATER ALWAYS ABSORBS the lesser. That is a reasonably well-accepted fact. England has always had a greater land area and a much larger population than Scotland, so the outcome of any union was perhaps inevitable.

It seems strange that the freedom that every nation has battled for since the dawn of time should, in Scotland's case, when that freedom was nullified, be decided on the stroke of a pen. Well, not only a pen, but a substantial amount of money changing hands in a surreptitious manner.

'We are bought and sold for English gold', wrote Burns. The bankruptcy caused by the Darien Scheme was very much a deciding factor in the Union, and yet much of that disaster was caused by English intervention – or lack of it when it was really needed.

The people of Scotland were firmly against the Union, of course, resulting in riots in the streets of Glasgow and Edinburgh. But they had no say in the outcome. Some of the great and good did do their best to preserve the independence of the ancient northern realm – particularly Andrew Fletcher of Saltoun, a man remembered for his loyalty. His home was Saltoun Hall in East Lothian; originally an old fortified building, but modernised and extended in the early 19th century. It is still a private house. Fletcher was buried in the family vault in the church of the nearby village of East Saltoun. The site is ancient. The original building was a dependency of Dryburgh Abbey, but today's Gothic-style building, with a tower and 90ft-high spire, is mostly from 1805. Every year, a commemoration of Fletcher's work is held in the village.

Scotland's last parliament rose on 25 March 1707, never to meet again until 1999. It had seen impassioned pleas in defence of liberty by the Duke of Hamilton (who was to change sides and betray his people at the eleventh hour) and Lord Belhaven. Belhaven had made a speech in which he stated that the Scots were now slaves forever, and that the Union was an entire surrender. He actually dropped to his knees in tears, begging fellow-peers not to betray their country. He was answered by the pro-Union Earl of Marchmont, who said sneeringly, 'Behold, I dreamed, and lo, when I awoke, I found it was a dream.' The articles of the Union were pushed through.

The Cameronians marched into the town of Dumfries, and at the market cross they burned a copy of the articles, along with a list of the commissioners who signed it. They intended to march on Edinburgh but were betrayed by spies and the insurrection petered out.

Many of the articles of Union have since been broken or disregarded. One of these was Article 16, which stated that there should always be a separate mint in Scotland. Although the coinage was to be the same in both countries, Scots coins struck at the mint in Edinburgh were distinguished by the addition of an 'e' beneath the portrait of Queen Anne. For some reason, there were no identification marks on coins struck in London. Crowns, half-crowns, shillings and six-pences were struck in 1707 and 1708, but by 1709 only half-crowns and shillings were produced. These were the last coins struck in Scotland. The mint then remained dormant and was abolished in 1817, the building finally being demolished in 1877.

The first coins in Scotland were struck in the reign of David 1 in 1136, and for 600 years each king or queen had produced their own.

The Hunterian Museum in Glasgow University has a large collection, which is usually on show, and many smaller museums in Scotland have collections of some sort. I love to look over these remnants from the many different ages of our history, especially the early 'hammered' coins – made simply by striking bullion with a hammer and die – and try to imagine the hands that once held them. Wallace? Bruce? Mary Queen of Scots? Times when Scotland really was Scotland.

CHAPTER THIRTY

Towering reminder of 'Bobbing John'

Recorded as a draw, a clash in the Ochil Hills is recalled by a visit to the Earl of Mar's finely restored birthplace.

THE EARL OF MAR, who led the Jacobite forces at the Battle of Sheriffmuir in 1715, was commonly known as 'Bobbing John' due to his ability to duck and dive, or to change sides as the climate suited.

He was born in Alloa Tower, which was built in the reign of David II, between 1360 and 1380. It stands a little east of Alloa town centre and signposts to it have been erected recently. The tower is an imposing structure. Its site is not particularly defensive, but the walls are ten feet thick, and the building itself is the epitome of lordly power and strength, rising some 65 feet above the surrounding countryside. It is open to visitors from April to September.

The Battle of Sheriffmuir was fought on the western shoulder of the Ochil Hills, a little above Dunblane. The battle has gone down in our history books as a draw, both sides managing to overcome one wing of the other, with the outcome that neither side was too sure who was the victor. Casualties were equal on both sides too. This led to the penning of the sarcastic lines,

> There's some say that we won, And some say that they won, And some say that none won at a' man, But of one thing I'm sure, That at Sheriffmuir, A battle there was, that I saw, man, And we ran and they ran, And they ran and we ran, And we ran, and they ran awa' man.

The easiest way to visit the battlefield is by taking the unclassified road, signposted Sheriffmuir, from the large roundabout in Dunblane that was on the route of the old A9 (the town has now been bypassed by a more modern stretch). This runs right through the battle site and meets the A9 again further north at Blackford.

Crossing the battlefield, you find a large memorial cairn at the roadside – the Clan MacRae stone, dedicated to the men of that clan who fought at Sheriffmuir. It bears an inscription in English and Gaelic. The Gaelic for MacRae is *MacRath*, or 'Son of Grace', and probably has an ecclesiastical origin.

A path leads down the side of the cairn to the Gathering Stone of the Clans. There is usually a signpost marking the way, but it was missing at time of writing. The Highlanders who took part in the battle are said to have met here to whet their dirks and before the fight – not an unreasonable assumption. The stone is enclosed by an iron grating, with a brass plate attached, gifted by a Mr Stirling of Kippendavie in 1840. North of the battlefield is the Sheriffmuir Inn, which hosts commemorations of the battle.

There are some grand viewpoints in this vicinity, and short drives will give vistas over Strathallan and the valley of the Forth, the landscape of the Ochils having an almost Highland quality that belies its proximity to the central belt.

The Earl of Mar is usually said in our history books to have commanded the forces of 'The Pretender' at Sheriffmuir. This shows how history is written by the winners, and details twisted to suit. James VIII was no 'pretender'. He was the legitimate heir to the thrones of Britain, but it was the Hanoverian George I who had become king due to political and religious manoeuvring, even though there was many dozens closer in bloodline than the German.

The fact that James is often referred to as 'The Pretender', as if he were some sort of imposter, shows how effectively the propaganda machinery of the day operated.

CHAPTER THIRTY-ONE

Wade's network of roads

Impressive though it is, General Wade's network of roads
represents the end of a way of life in the Highlands.

EVERY TIME I DRIVE the route of one of General Wade's roads, I
marvel at the sweat and toil that went into their construction.
Hundreds of miles of roads were built – Wade's programme itself
was responsible for around 250 miles of construction – and a great
number of rivers and burns bridged, all in the days before heavy
machinery, when the average worker had to use a shovel and
wheelbarrow.

Part of me is saddened, though, as these roads also represent the
end of the traditional Highland way of life; their initial purpose was
the pacification of the unruly Highlands by a London government.

Probably Wade's most famous road was his route north from
Dunkeld to Inverness, crossing the Grampians. Much of this road
has been superseded by the modern A9.

Another road commenced at Crieff, ran through the Sma' Glen
to Aberfeldy, and crossed the River Tay by what is probably
Wade's finest bridge, which today still carries motor traffic. This
bridge was completed in 1735 and its total cost was around
£4,000. Its five arches are described as 'elegant and substantial' by
various guidebooks.

At one end of the bridge stands the Black Watch Monument,
built in 1887 to commemorate the inauguration of the Black Watch
Regiment in October 1739. The Black Watch was actually raised
to keep an eye on the Highlands, to give early warning of any sign
of uprising against the Hanoverian monarchy ruling Scotland from
London.

The road from Aberfeldy continued north over the Perthshire
hills by way of Tummel – the bridge there is also a work of Wade

– and connected with the main north route at Dalnacardoch in Glen Garry, a little below the Drumochter Pass. General Wade had a hut at Dalnacardoch, which eventually became an inn, and in later years Bonnie Prince Charlie spent a night within its walls.

On the completion of this section of road, an eight-foot-high pillar of stone was raised. It stands about two miles north-west of Dalnacardoch, in a lovely setting. It has carved upon it the date 1729, and it is known locally as 'The Wade Stone'. Wade was a man of great stature, and he managed to reach up and place a coin on the top of the stone. He revisited the site a year later, and was surprised when he found the coin was still there.

North of the Drumochter Pass, a spur forked west from the main north-south route to Inverness, and cut over to the side of Loch Ness by the famous Corrieyairack Pass. The road there reached the top of the 2,500ft pass in a series of steep zigzags. This spur connected with the military road Wade constructed between Fort William and Inverness.

The main motor road today between these two towns follows the line of Wade's original, excepting the Loch Ness stretch. Wade's road was on the loch's south side, whereas the modern road follows its north side.

From the spur at Drumochter, the main route north passes the ruins of Ruthven Barracks at Kingussie. These barracks were also the work of General Wade.

Wade was relieved of his command in Scotland in 1740 but played a military role in later campaigns, including the '45 rising. He died in Bath in 1748, aged 75, and was buried in Westminster Abbey.

The best known of his successors was General Caulfield, who continued the road-building programme. He supposedly penned the famous lines:

> If you'd seen these roads before they were made,
> You'd lift up your hands, and bless General Wade.

By the end of the 18th century, there were 1,103 miles of these roads. They opened up the Highlands to travellers from the south – and their foreign influences – but as already mentioned, it was a double-edged sword, as the improvement in communications also ended much of the Highland way of life.

CHAPTER THIRTY-TWO

A great march that wasn't

*When the Stewart flag was raised, it marked the beginning
of an audacious incursion into England. But the promised
Jacobite support was not to be.*

AFTER THE RAISING of the standard of the Stewarts at Glenfinnan,
the Jacobites' march south began. There is today a visitor centre at
Glenfinnan, as well as an older tower surmounted by the statue of
a Highlander, but the actual site where the deed took place is on
the opposite side of the River Finnan, up by the railway track,
where a carved stone marks the spot.

The first action of the '45 took place at Highbridge, where a
handful of Jacobites panicked two divisions of Redcoats into flight
and capture. A cairn beside the ruined bridge, near modern Spean
Bridge, marks the site. The Highlanders then crossed the
Corrieyairack, following the route of the A9 south. Charles stayed
at the Salutation Hotel in Perth – which still trades, and boasts a
plaque recalling its princely guest.

The Forth was crossed at the Bridge of Frew, and a march was
made on Edinburgh, where Charles took quarters at Holyrood
Palace. Holyrood is open to the public, and you can walk the cor-
ridors and see rooms that Charles would recognise.

The Battle of Prestonpans was fought at this time. In the town,
there is a cairn marking the site, and a pyramid-mound, with
storyboards on its summit, which offers a magnificent view of the
battle area.

The march to the Border continued; the Esk was crossed; and
Carlisle besieged. During the siege, Charles stayed in the village of
Brampton, some 10 miles east. His headquarters are now a shoe
shop, with a plaque testifying the royal connection on the outside
wall. On the fall of Carlisle, the prince took up quarters in a house

which has today been replaced by a town-centre Marks & Spencer store. Looking up to first-floor level, you will see there is a plaque telling of Charles' stay.

The Jacobite army continued south, marching along the line of the A6, through Penrith. Charles stayed at what is now the George Hotel. Crossing Shap summit, the army rested at Kendal. Next halt was at Lancaster, and Charles's HQ there is now the Conservative Club in Church Street.

On reaching Preston, the army deliberately crossed the River Ribble, as no Scots army had ever done so before while marching south; it was seen as a good omen for the project. Charles stayed in a building in the Strait Shambles, which now lies under the modern Guildhall.

But it was around this time that the truth began to dawn – English Jacobitism failed to provide active backing. There may have been promises of large-scale support, but when push came to shove, it seemed sympathisers in England preferred to take the back seat in any attempts to reinstate the House of Stewart.

From Preston, the Jacobites entered Wigan, Charles staying at the Manor House in Bishopsgate. This building has gone, but its replacement bears a plaque. Then came Manchester, where at least there was some support, and the new followers were formed into what became known as 'the Manchester Regiment'.

The army moved on apace, and one can only marvel at the distances covered by men carrying all their weaponry and goods on their backs. They forded the Mersey at Stockport; their line of march then took them through Macclesfield, Leek, and on to Ashbourne. Eventually Derby was reached, where the advance guard walked into the town and demanded quarters for 9,000 men.

Charles took up quarters in Exeter House in Full Street. This building has now gone, but an equestrian statue of Charles marks its site. This is the only statue of the Bonnie Prince in either England or Scotland. In Derby, the Jacobites were out of the rolling hills of the north of England and into the softer underbelly of the south. London was little more than 100 miles off.

The advance guard secured the bridge over the Trent at Swarkstone, six miles south of Derby. It was the furthest point south the army reached. A visit to this bridge today is a cause for contemplation of what might have been. There was panic in London, but some key Jacobites believed false information regarding the strength of forces being set against them. The decision was made to retire to Scotland.

At the rate they had travelled that far, a march of four days would have seen the Jacobites in London.

It was only on the retreat, seeing landmarks they recognised, that the rank and file realised they were heading north, not south. Consternation reigned. If the clansmen had had their say, they would have marched on to London, and damned be to any of the forces King George sent against them.

CHAPTER THIRTY-THREE

The fugitive prince

Loyalty marked the trail of the biggest manhunt in Highland history, as Charles headed eastwards over the sea to Skye.

CULLODEN HAD BEEN LOST and won; Charles's escape route took him through the country to the south of Loch Ness. One of his first halts was at Invergarry Castle. The castle was later blown up by Cumberland's vengeful Hanoverians, but its gaunt ruins still stand atop the 'Raven's Rock' or, in Gaelic, *Creag an Fhitich*.

This was also the battle cry of the MacDonells of Glengarry, showing their inherent love for their native heath. The castle stands on the western shore of Loch Oich, close to the A82, in the grounds of a hotel.

From here, moving south and west, Charles travelled through the *Mile Dorcha* – the 'Dark Mile' – which links Loch Lochy and Loch Arkaig. The name came from the gloom of the heavy tree cover, but modern road upgrading and forestry has lessened the original effect.

The country running west from here is steeped in the legend surrounding the Prince's flight. The hills were crossed and recrossed to escape the clutches of the Redcoats. Charles was an early Munro bagger, spending a night out on the summit of Sgurr Thuilm, above the head of Glen Finnan, where the Royal Standard of the Stewarts had fluttered only months before.

The ordinary clansmen did not see Culloden as the end of the campaign. As far as they were concerned it was simply the first battle they had lost. They regrouped at Ruthven Barracks, but the order to disperse destroyed their hopes.

Ruthven Barracks, built by the government to control this area, stand complete to the wallhead, a little to the east of the A9, just south of Kingussie. The barracks had been the scene of earlier actions of the '45. The mound upon which they stand was the site of a medieval castle owned by the Comyn family at the time of Bruce. The barracks are a familiar sight to drivers commuting this main north-south route.

Tracing the routes that Charles took during his flight cannot fail to impress. 20 and 30-mile treks were undertaken in usually wet weather and with poor rations; an astonishing feat, covering some of Scotland's roughest terrain. Even Charles's hardy companions, bred to the hills, commented on his ability to adapt.

To escape Cumberland's wrath, Charles spent much time sailing and wandering the Outer Isles but, inevitably, escape became essential. This is where Flora MacDonald enters the story. Flora was instrumental in smuggling Charles 'Over the sea to Skye'. The journey was eastward to Skye and not, as many imagine, west-wards from the mainland. Landfall was made on the Trotternish peninsula at a location near Monkstadt, still shown on maps as 'Prince Charles's Point'.

Flora MacDonald died in 1790 and, strangely, she is buried not far from where that landfall was made. At Kilmuir on Score Bay, a large Celtic cross marks her last resting place. The original cross was erected in 1871, but fell in a storm in December 1873. The current cross, rising to a height of 28½ft, was erected in 1880. The fallen cross still lies in the grass beside its successor.

A tangible reminder of the loyalty that the people of the Highlands felt for Charles can be visited in Glen Moriston, where the Rivers Doe and Moriston meet, close to the A887. Here a cairn bears a plaque which states:

At this spot in 1746 died Roderick MacKenzie, an officer in the army of Prince Charles Edward Stewart. Of the same size and similar resemblance to his Royal Prince, when surrounded and overpowered by the troops of the Duke of Cumberland gallantly died in attempting to save his fugitive leader from further pursuit.

Apparently, when MacKenzie was cut down he exclaimed: 'You have slain your Prince!' and this threw the Hanoverian forces off the scent for a while, allowing Charles a well-needed breathing space from pursuit.

Charles eventually left Scotland on 20 September 1746, sailing from Loch nan Uamh, 'the Loch of the Caves'. A cairn erected in 1956 marks the spot. It stands on the shore beside the A830 Mallaig road, and a lay-by just past the cairn allows parking.

CHAPTER THIRTY-FOUR

The forts built to pacify the 'rebels'

After their regime came close to toppling, Hanoverian response to the '45 was predictable – to ensure it did not happen again.

THE THREE MAIN FORTS built by the London government for the pacification of the Highlands of Scotland were all in Glen Mor, the Great Glen, which divides Scotland along the route of the Caledonian Canal.

Starting in the south-west we have Fort William, today the principal town of Lochaber. This area was originally called Inverlochy, the name surviving in the medieval castle. General Monck built an earthen walled fortress here in 1655, but it was replaced by a smaller stone structure in July 1690, and named Fort William after William of Orange. It had a triangular form, with ditch, glacis and ravelin, a bombproof magazine, two bastions mounting 15 cannon, and accommodation for 104 men. During the '45, the Jacobites tried unsuccessfully to capture the fort, mounting their own cannon on an eminence known as the Rock. The government sold the fort in 1860 to a Mrs Campbell of Monzie, and it was demolished in 1894 to make way for the new West Highland Railway.

The West Highland Museum in Fort William has preserved the fort's panelling of 1707, which was formerly in the house of the governor. The original gateway was re-erected in 1896 at the Craigs, the town's old cemetery. The Rock stands just west of this gate. Local Gaelic speakers still refer to the town as *An Gearasdan* – The Garrison.

As the town was named Fort William after a man who had a thinly disguised hatred of Scotland and its people, and the garrison was built to cow the people of this district, I would love to see the native name of Inverlochy creep back into existence.

Fort Augustus, 32 miles to the north-east of Fort William, was originally known as *Cilla-chuimein*, or *Kilcummin*, the Cell of Cumin, a former abbot of Iona. Its name change took place in 1716, when the fort was built to try to pacify the surrounding clans. It stood on a peninsula with the River Oich on its north-west, the Tarff on its south-east, and the deep waters of Loch Ness fronting it.

General Wade enlarged the fort in 1730, and named it Fort Augustus as a compliment to William Augustus, Duke of Cumberland. The Duke of Cumberland was the man responsible for the murder, rape and theft perpetrated against the people of Scotland after Culloden.

The fort was in the form of a square, with accommodation for 300 men. It had a bastion at each angle, mounting 12 six-pound guns, and was surrounded by a ditch. The Jacobites attacked the fort in March 1746. A shell fired by a Jacobite cannon from neighbouring high ground hit the powder magazine and caused a huge explosion.

The fort was later restored, and remained in service till 1857, when it was sold to Lord Lovat for £5,000. He donated it to the Fathers of the English Benedictine Congregation in 1876, and the Abbey, which still stands there today, is built on the fort's ruins.

To the north-east again, guarding the approaches to Glen Mor from that direction, stands Fort George, some 10 miles north-east of Inverness. It was named after the Hanoverian King George, and was constructed three years after the '45 at a cost of £160,000, which was a vast sum for those days.

It covers 16 acres of ground with its polygonal lines, has six bastions and is defended on its land side by a ditch, the other side being protected by the Moray Firth. The vital buildings were designed to be bomb-proof, and it has accommodation for 1,600 men. It became the headquarters of the Seaforth Highlanders, then the Queen's Own Highlanders. The fort, still complete, has a museum and is open to the public.

The spit of land that Fort George stands upon at Ardersier juts out to almost meet Chanonry Point in the Black Isle, at the opposite side of the Moray Firth, and is an ideal spot from which to view the dolphins and porpoises that inhabit the waters.

It is pleasing that I can finish by recommending Fort George as a place to view wildlife, and that its role as subjugator of the people of the Highlands – alongside other forts – is now defunct.

CHAPTER THIRTY-FIVE

From farming to medicine

It was the sheer brilliance of their pioneering minds that took the Hunters from their humble East Kilbride farm. Their influence on surgery is still felt today.

WHEN MOST PEOPLE THINK of the Enlightenment they imagine Edinburgh, as the centre of thinking which made such progressive advances in science and the arts possible. But this was not always the case.

Two of the country's most famous medical pioneers were the brothers John and William Hunter, born into a family that farmed at Long Calderwood, near what was then the village of East Kilbride.

Their parents, John and Agnes, had a family of 10 children and scratched a living farming oats, barley and kail on their 75 acres. Times were hard. Three of the children died in childhood, four died in their youth, and only John, William and one sister survived to adulthood.

Although born into humble stock, John remembered in later life: 'I wanted to know all about the clouds and grasses, why the leaves changed colour in autumn. I watched the ants, bees, birds, tadpoles and worms. I pestered people with questions about which nobody knew or cared about.'

William was apprenticed to a local surgeon, and quickly made a name for himself with his radical new ideas in medicine. He eventually moved to London and began a school of anatomy. His fame steadily increased. Younger brother John, with his huge interest in biology, decided to leave the farm and join his eminent brother in London. He borrowed one of the farm's plough horses and rode it all the way.

John and William, like many siblings, did not really get along when they were together and there was often friction. But there was also a brilliance in both of their minds that yielded discoveries which still affect modern surgery and anatomy today.

William was a phenomenal collector of curios and artefacts and amassed a fascinating collection, which he eventually bequeathed to Glasgow University in 1783. This forms the basis of the famous Hunterian Museum, within the University, which is open to the public. Most notable is its collection of coins, a huge percentage of which are Scottish in origin.

The Hunter brothers were two of the most famous men in London in their time. Other great thinkers flocked to hear their theories and discoveries.

They died, as they were born, 10 years apart, and are buried within Westminster Abbey. The farmhouse where they were born was a working farm till the 1960s, but has now been swallowed up by the ever-expanding new town of East Kilbride. It is a grade A listed building and, fortunately, has been converted into a museum. There are computer terminals that you can use to explore the human body, audio-visual films describing the lives of the Hunters, and a collection of surgical instruments used in their time – plenty to catch the attention of adults and children alike.

The museum is open midday to 4pm weekdays, midday to 5pm weekends, 1 April till 30 September. Admission is currently free. Hunter House, as the farm is now called, stands on Maxwellton Road in the Calderwood area of East Kilbride.

There is another Hunter connection elsewhere within East Kilbride. A large sandstone memorial was erected to the brothers in 1937, on the edge of the original village. This memorial now stands beside Priestknowe Roundabout and its inscription sums up their careers succinctly:

To the memory of the brothers William Hunter 1718–1783 and John Hunter 1728–1793. They were born at Long

Calderwood and died in London after attaining the highest eminence in the sciences of medicine and biology. Their names will be held in reverent remembrance by a grateful posterity to all generations.

CHAPTER THIRTY-SIX

The warrior test

The mists of time may have obscured the colourful lives of legendary Celtic leader Finn MacCool and the bard Ossian, but they have left their marks all around the Highlands.

THE TALES OF OSSIAN were published by James MacPherson in the 1760s. MacPherson claimed that he had found an original manuscript of Ossian's work, telling the tales of warriors from Dark Age Scotland. These stories were first hailed as Scotland's equivalent to the works of Homer, but then suspicion grew that they were a fake. MacPherson's claim that he had an original manuscript was apparently false, but it certainly seems that he had gathered his material from the folk memory of the people of the Highlands of Scotland. In MacPherson's work, Ossian recounted the life of the legendary Finn MacCool, who will be familiar to most Scots through placenames such as Fingal's Cave on the island of Staffa. Finn, or in Gaelic, Fionn, led a band of warriors called the Fianna.

There are many sites in northern Scotland that bear an association with these perhaps mythical heroes. The site with the most Fianna connections seems to be Glen Lyon in Perthshire – the longest glen in Scotland. There is a chain of ancient forts the length of the glen, and they are still visible today.

Legend has it that Finn had two dogs, wolfhounds named Bran and Sceolang, which he used to tether to the Bhacain, a stone shaped like a dog's head standing by the road near the Caisteal Coin-a-Bhacain, the Castle of the Dog's Stake, in the upper reaches of the glen.

Any youth who wanted to join the ranks of the Fianna had first to prove himself by lifting the Bodach Chraig Fianna, a heavy, rounded stone, up to a nearby rock ledge. Many years ago I made the attempt. I managed to at least raise it, but the sheer weight made walking impossible. Older now, and stronger, if not wiser, I should return to see if I am now fit to join the ranks of the warriors of Ossian and Finn's day!

There are several tales centred on Finn's death, and a standing stone behind the school in Killin, at the head of Loch Tay, is said to mark his burial place. But when the grave was opened some 200 years ago, no skeleton was found.

Other accounts tell of Finn surrounded by his warriors, sleeping in a cavern in Skye. Once a man stumbled upon the cave by accident and found them slumbering within. They were giants with huge shields and spears, Finn in the centre, the largest of all these mighty warriors, all waiting for the day when their country would call upon them and they would wake to fight again.

High on the north face of Aonach Dubh in Glen Coe is the huge, black, keyhole-shaped slit of Ossian's Cave. It can be seen from the road at Loch Achtriochtan, and it does look like a huge keyhole carved into the rock. It is reached by a rock climb known as Ossian's Ladder. The cave runs with water and has a steeply sloping floor, so it is unlikely Ossian ever really occupied it.

The Hermitage, a National Trust for Scotland property on the A9 near Dunkeld, was formerly known as Ossian's Hall. It stands above a waterfall on the River Braan, and was originally lined with mirrors. The building somehow magnifies the noise of the falls in time of spate, and that, coupled with the reflections of rushing water in the multitude of mirrors, made it a hall fit for a Fingalian hero.

If you are driving the A9 and happen to be passing after heavy rain, it is well worth stopping and enjoying the half-mile or so of forest path leading to The Hermitage and taking in the noise and grandeur created by the design of the building. This area has an almost magical feel, conjuring images of fairies and other such things kids find fascinating, which is worth bearing in mind if you are driving your metal box on wheels with bored little ones.

Ossian's end came at the Sma' Glen, which carries the A822 north of Crieff. A large boulder between the road and the River Almond is said to be his gravestone, but it has been moved from its original site. It is about eight feet high and five feet broad. When it was moved by soldiers in 1728, to make way for one of General Wade's military roads, a cavity about two feet square was found underneath, lined with stone slabs. It contained some bones and ashes.

It is reported that many of the local people came from miles around with pipes playing, carried away the bones and deposited them in a stone circle in western Glenalmond, where they 'might never more be disturbed by mortal feet or hands'.

It seems our more recent ancestors did not like to see the last resting place of one of our ancient warriors being disturbed. Wordsworth, a well-known fan of Ossianic poetry, wrote of this incident:

The separation that is here. Is of the grave and of austere. Yet happy feelings of the dead; And, therefore, it is rightly said, That Ossian, last of all his race. Lies buried in this lonely place.

CHAPTER THIRTY-SEVEN

Burns shed a tear for Wallace

The story of how Wallace hid in Leglen Wood beside the River Ayr deeply affected the Bard – and later led to the greatest Scots battle hymn ever written.

EVERY TIME I LOOK at images of Burns I feel we are not seeing the 'real' man. In many portraits he appears almost effeminate, as if he has been sanitised in some way. I imagine the real Burns, used to hard farm labour, would have been the type of man you would not like to give you a punch!

There are all the obvious sites with Burns connections you can visit – his birthplace cottage at Alloway; the bridge over the River Doon, where the witches snatched the tail from Tam's grey mare; the Globe Inn in Dumfries, which is essentially unchanged since Burns's day.

But there are other, lesser-known sites that I find equally poignant. One such is Leglen Wood. When Burns was a boy he was regaled with stories of the exploits of William Wallace. He was familiar with Blind Harry's book on the deeds of Wallace, a work written in the late 1400s and the second biggest selling book ever in Scotland (number one being the Bible).

Harry's book tells how Wallace hid from pursuers in Leglen Wood on the River Ayr. In later life, Burns recalled how Wallace's story caused him to shed a tear, and he stated that when he was a boy he 'chose a fine summer Sunday, the only day of the week in my power, and walked the half-a-dozen miles to pay my respects to the Leglen Wood with as much devout enthusiasm as ever Pilgrim did to Lorreto.'

Like many a child, Burns explored all the wood's secret places, imagining Wallace with his mighty sword upon his back, skulking in the caves or moving stealthily through the undergrowth.

Burns also stated that he wished that one day he would be enough of a rhymer to be able to write a song that did justice to the deeds of Wallace. Burns's early forays into Leglen Wood were to result in the lyrics of 'Scots Wha Hae', his words welded onto an old soldiers' marching song dating back to the time of the Wars of Independence. It seems amazing that this tune, so familiar to Scots today, was also well known to Wallace and Bruce. It was even played to Joan of Arc at the siege of Orleans by her famous Garde d'Ecosse. Too often 'Scots Wha Hae' is played as a dirge, when it should really be hammered out with vigour, befitting the martial hymn that it is.

Burns stated that: 'The story of Wallace poured a Scottish prejudice in my veins which will boil along there until the floodgates of life shut in eternal rest.'

A cairn was erected in Leglen Wood in 1929, built in memory of both Wallace and Burns. If you would like to visit this cairn, in a site familiar to two of Scotland's greatest heroes, you should take the A77 running east of the town of Ayr. At the roundabout with the exit westwards marked 'Ayr north', take the route eastwards on the B743 towards Mossblown. A little further along this road, a side turning south takes you into the grounds of Auchencruive Agricultural College. The road crosses the River Ayr by means of Oswald's Bridge, and directly on your right stands the cairn amongst the trees of the wood.

Only a dozen miles further south on the A77 is the village of Kirkoswald. The little kirk here, from which the village takes its name, is ancient. A wander around the graveyards will reveal the last resting place of Burns's grandparents, and those of Burns's two great cronies, Tam O'Shanter and Souter Johnnie.

Souter Johnnie's cottage in the village is open as a museum.

Within the now rootless church is an old carved stone font. It is believed locally that Robert the Bruce, born at nearby Turnberry Castle, was baptised in it.

CHAPTER THIRTY-EIGHT

Waterways that kept Scotland moving

*Our Lowland canals still stand as testimony
to the iron men who created them.*

THE FORTH AND CLYDE CANAL, which runs from Grangemouth in the east to Bowling in the west, was begun in 1768. The Battle of Falkirk, the field of which is not too far from the canal, had been fought between the Jacobites and Hanoverians only 22 years before, in 1746. It is strange that the industrial revolution came so close on the heels to the days of battles with targe and claymore in central Scotland.

The Forth and Clyde was finished in 1790. When you consider that all its construction, all its building of dykes, all the digging, all the fording of rivers and streams, had to be done by hand, it becomes all the more impressive. No JCBs in those days – the workmen used nothing more than wheelbarrows and spades.

I had always intended to walk the canal end to end, and I did it while training for the 'Walk for Wallace', where I walked to London from Glasgow to commemorate the 700th anniversary of the murder of our patriot hero. The canal is 35 miles long but, as you can imagine, there is little gradient, and the towpaths are in a tolerable state.

The canal does reach 156ft above sea level near Castlecary, achieved by the passage of various locks. It is on average 56ft wide on its surface, 27ft wide at the bottom, and is roughly 10ft deep over its entire course.

It closely follows the Roman Antonine Wall along almost its entire length, which shows how even our earliest visitors were wise to this easily navigable route over the narrow waist of our land.

The Forth and Clyde sends off a spur into the very heart of Glasgow, terminating 2.75 miles later at the city's Port Dundas. The old warehouses here are now converted into flats, and if you are in Glasgow and have a spare hour or two, you can do worse than park at the basin and go for a stroll along the banks. It is astonishing the amount of wildfowl nesting along the route, considering the proximity of the canal to houses and factories.

The Union Canal was opened in 1822, after only four years of work. Four years? That is extraordinary considering the engineering complexity that it must have entailed, never mind the many millions of tonnes of soil and rock that were moved in its construction. Walking its length will soon bring the scale of the achievement home to you. It runs from Port Hopetoun, at the west of Edinburgh, to join with the Forth and Clyde a mile and a half south-west of Falkirk. It covers 31½ miles during its course and its construction made it feasible to take passengers and goods by canal from Glasgow to Edinburgh, albeit via Falkirk.

The Union Canal boasts a tunnel, 700 yards in length, taking it through a hill south of Falkirk. This tunnel is carved through solid rock, and it must have taken many thousands of man-hours to complete it.

I once met a man in passing who told me he worked on the upkeep of the Union Canal. I asked him a couple of questions, and I still vividly recall his answers: Were any items of interest found when they were checking the canal bed, I asked; 'Whisky bottles,' came the reply. 'Thousands and thousands of them.'

It seems the bargees, with little else to do other than steer a horse-drawn barge, liked their whisky – and the empties were simply slung overboard.

My other question was, what happens when it rains really heavily on only one end of the canal?

He told me it takes three days for the canal, through its own devices, to level out. There is no current flow, but the canal does have ducts to run off excess water and prevent overflow.

Recently, work was undertaken to raise the level of the M8 over the Union Canal, and the A80 over the Forth and Clyde, to make them navigable again. Earlier planners ran the roads too close to the surface, leaving insufficient clearance for traffic. It is good these inland waterways will once again be put to use – even if only for pleasure craft. It is a fitting testimony at least to the men who strained muscles working in their construction. It would be a shame if all that back-breaking work had simply been allowed to deteriorate.

CHAPTER THIRTY-NINE

Martyrs in the name of the people

They are almost forgotten, but while the flame of the French Revolution was burning bright, Scotland's radicals were found guilty of sedition and transported to Botany Bay.

ONE FACT WORTH REMEMBERING is that the *Press and Journal* is the oldest surviving newspaper on the planet. This may come in handy for a pub quiz one day! The next eldest in succession were Glasgow's *Herald*, then the London *Times*.

The spread of the printed word created a great interest in radical ideas among the lower classes in Scotland, especially as many newspapers and journals were political and against the policies of the day. The most meteoric and best known of the radicals of this period was Thomas Muir (1765–1799).

Muir was the son of a Glasgow merchant. The family built themselves a house, named Huntershill, in the Bishopbriggs area of Glasgow in 1770, and Muir was raised there. The house still stands in Crowhill Road, near Bishopbriggs Railway Station. It has been extended, and is used as a pavilion for the nearby playing fields, but the original building in the centre of the extensions looks very much as it did when built.

Muir studied and practised law in Glasgow and Edinburgh, eventually becoming a noted reformer connected with the Friends of the People and the United Irishmen. His influence in Scotland coincided with revolutionary events in France. He was eventually taken into custody on 4 August 1793, and was tried in Edinburgh on 30–31 August for libel and making seditious speeches. To the shock of many, he was given the harsh sentence of 14 years transportation to Australia's Botany Bay.

He escaped in 1796, fleeing to France, where he was regarded as a hero and granted citizenship. He died there on 26 January 1799, in Chantily, while he was still only 33.

On the opposite side of Crowhill Road from Huntershill House stands a coffee shop and garden centre. A plaque on the front wall of this garden centre tells the story of Muir's life.

A memorial cairn was also erected in 1996, bearing a bust of Muir, and the following lines:

> I have devoted myself to the cause of the people. It is a good cause. It shall ultimately prevail. It shall finally triumph.
>
> Damned from this mansion to a foreign land, To waste his days of gay and sprightly youth And all for sowing with a liberal hand the seed of that seditious libel truth.

Behind this cairn stands an iron Martyrs' Gate bearing plaques in remembrance of Maurice Margarot, transported for 14 years for sedition in 1793, along with the Rev. Thomas Fyshe Palmer (seven years), William Skirving (14 years) and Joseph Gerrald (14 years).

A tall obelisk to Muir's memory stands in the old Calton Cemetery in Edinburgh, but it is not often mentioned in guide-books to the city. It seems Muir is still regarded as *persona non grata* in many quarters due to his revolutionary beliefs.

William Skirving was a contemporary of Muir, and hailed from Fife. The Abbot's House in Dunfermline has a room dedicated to his memory. This room contains a life-size figure of Skirving sitting at a table, based on contemporary drawings.

The Abbot's House also contains a commemorative handker-chief printed with the names of Muir, Skirving and Palmer. This handkerchief was originally issued in Australia.

The Abbot's House is a 16th-century building and, as its name suggests, was constructed for the Abbots of Dunfermline Abbey. It stands hard against the northern side of the Abbey Churchyard, with a museum, shop and cafe within, and is harled in an attractive pink finish. No visitor to Dunfermline should miss it – or any of the town's other historic attractions, such as the tomb of Robert the Bruce, the remains of Malcolm Canmore's tower, and St Margaret's Cave – all within a short walking distance of one another.

CHAPTER FORTY

Amazing home of Sir Walter

The Borders were always special for Sir Walter Scott, who built and furnished his famous home at Abbotsford with the relics of Scottish history.

ANYONE INTERESTED in Sir Walter Scott must visit Abbotsford, Scott's house on the River Tweed, near Melrose. It is signposted from the main road running between Melrose and Galashiels.

Scott purchased the site in 1811. It originally bore the name of Cartleyhole, or the even less attractive Clartyhole. Scott knew the nearby shallows of the Tweed had once been used as a crossing point by the monks of Melrose Abbey, and he changed the name to Abbotsford.

Between 1817 and 1821 he built the present stately baronial mansion. Many of its parts are copies of famous architectural objects, such as a gateway from Linlithgow Palace, a portal from the Edinburgh Old Tolbooth, a roof from Rosslyn Chapel, a mantel-piece from Melrose Abbey and oak-work from Holyrood Palace.

The house is filled with a wealth of objects from every era of Scottish history. Among the bits and pieces covering the walls are Rob Roy's basket-hilted broadsword and dirk; a crucifix that belonged to Mary Queen of Scots; and copies of some candlesticks that belonged to Robert the Bruce. There are other notable attractions, such as some of the personal items of Napoleon Bonaparte. Sir Walter was a great collector of Scottish artefacts, but he was also the recipient of numerous gifts from admirers.

Abbotsford House is open to the public, and is still owned and run by Sir Walter's direct descendants.

Many parts of Scotland bear a connection with Scott. He 'created' the Trossachs, his writings causing a plethora of visitors to the area, all eager to see the landscapes that he wrote about. The Trossachs continue to be a popular tourist destination.

When Scott visited Douglas Castle in southern Lanarkshire, tears rolled down his cheeks, so moved was he by this cradle of so much of Scotland's history. Douglas Castle was to be made famous as the model for his book *Castle Dangerous*, and it is still known by that name.

Scott had a key role in recovering Scotland's regalia – the crown, sceptre and sword of state. They had been consigned to a chest within Edinburgh Castle after the Treaty of Union. Scott's successful hunt can now be appreciated by visiting the 'Honours of Scotland' at the Castle. The regalia have now been joined by the Stone of Destiny, since its return from Westminster Abbey.

Scott's View is marked on most road maps. It is near Bemersyde on the B6356 near Melrose. High above the Tweed there is a lay-by with a panoramic vista over the Border country so beloved of Scott, with the Eildon Hills prominent in the foreground. Scott would often pause here to absorb so many sites prominent in Scotland's history. It is said that as Scott's body was being borne to its last resting place at Dryburgh Abbey, in a hearse drawn by his own horse, the horse stopped at the viewpoint as it had always done when Scott was alive. It paused for a moment, before trotting dutifully on, just as it had so many times before.

Dryburgh Abbey was founded in 1150, but it was badly damaged by invading English armies in 1322, 1385 and, finally, 1544. It is the last resting place of several members of Scott's family, together with J.G. Lockhart, Scott's biographer; Field Marshal Earl Haig; and the 11th Earl of Buchan, Scott's close friend, who was responsible for the giant statue of William Wallace that stands on the hillside near the Abbey ruins.

Walter Scott was very much a Unionist, but that has to be balanced out by the fact that he did so much to give back the Scottish people their history. A strange dichotomy.

CHAPTER FORTY-ONE

An empty landscape

On the side of Ben Lawers I found clusters of ruins, little bridges over burns, evidence of a once thriving community.

STARTING IN MY TEENS, I used to spend all my available free time wandering the hills of the Highlands, doing a bit of Munro-bagging while I learned the topography of Scotland, in every kind of weather – usually entailing a gallon of water down each boot.

Most of the empty glens I crossed would have a rickle of stones here, perhaps a gable-end still standing against the weather there, or I would notice the small patches of lighter green where there had once been cultivation.

On the north side of Ben Lawers, I discovered a cluster of ruins, little bridges over the burns, evidence that once there had been a thriving community. As I walked on I imagined someone in, say, Chicago, perhaps five generations an American, who was a hundred generations a Highlander, his family forced from their home at the spot I was just passing.

The eventual defeat of the Jacobite uprisings was the beginning of the end, with many of the chiefs desiring to distance themselves from anything remotely Highland and/or seditious, and the replacement of tenants with more profitable sheep. The empty glens are proof enough of this, but there are several sites bearing a special testament to those times. When the people from Glencalvie in Easter Ross were evicted from the land which they had farmed since their ancestors first came to those northern latitudes, they found temporary shelter in the churchyard of the Parliamentary Church at Croick in Strathcarron. The ministers, who should have done all in their power to help them, were under the sway of the landowners, and told the populace their misfortune was due to their own sinfulness, and that all their ills were brought on in retribution.

They spent a whole winter in the churchyard before their scattering, and during this time they scratched little messages on the window-panes of the church. One reads: 'Glencalvie people was in the churchyard, May 24, 1845.' Another reads: 'Glencalvie people – the wicked generation.'

The little church stands on the unclassified road that runs westwards from the village of Bonar Bridge up the length of Strathcarron.

Above the village of Golspie in Sutherland, high on Beinn a Bhragie, stands the famous statue of the infamous 1st Duke of Sutherland, created by the sculptor Chantrey. Much debate has taken place regarding this landmark, which can be seen for miles around. The duke was responsible for much of the 'improvement' from Cape Wrath to the Dornoch Firth. Many people want the statue to be retained as a reminder of the Highland Clearances, whereas others see it as an affront and wish it to be destroyed in order to erase his memory.

The duke's home was Dunrobin Castle (a fitting name), which stands to the north of Golspie. It had originally been a fortified structure, dating back to 1275, but by 1856 it had taken on the almost Disney-like aspect that can be seen today. It is open to the public at certain times during the summer.

It is strange that an Englishman, who had married into the Sutherland family to become duke, should have had the right to clear the indigenous Scottish people from their homes; people who had been on the land since the dawn of time. He probably had no more sympathy for the locals than the early settlers in Australia or America had for the natives there.

Driving to the far north of Scotland and taking one of the many straths that fan out from Lairg, the empty land before you is possibly the best testament to the Clearances. Scotland's loss, however, was to be to the benefit of the New World. A glance at the names on maps shows the impact of the colonial Scots. For example, Calgary was the name of a tiny settlement on Mull. Its name was carried by the locals to their new homes. Calgary is now a mighty Canadian city. The maps of the New World are scattered with familiar Scottish names.

CHAPTER FORTY-TWO

The iron road across heaven

It began as a way of tackling the Highland economy. It became a breathtaking 122-mile-long railway line from Glasgow to Fort William, over stunning moors and mountains, a gateway to the Hebrides.

THE INSPIRING VISION of a great railway line from a point somewhere on the west coast of the Highlands, communicating with the lucrative markets of the south and allowing a huge increase in trade, was a dream presented as a possible solution to the north's unemployment problems.

The proposition was welcomed by most of the landowners over whose ground the route would pass. Most seemed aware of the commercial gains increased transport would bring. The line would be the longest in Britain sanctioned by one Act of Parliament and, unusually, the whole project was granted to one group of contractors.

The vision turned into reality with the launch of the line in the autumn of 1889 at Craigendoran on the Clyde, 23 miles from Glasgow. Craigendoran had already been reached by the Helensburgh branch of the North British Railway.

The building of the railway cost £700,000 and it was opened in August 1894. It ran through the counties of Dunbarton, Perth, Argyll and Inverness to Fort William, opening up contact with 4,000 square miles of countryside that previously had little real communication with the central belt, other than by the most basic of roads. And what countryside! The railway crossed some of the most heavenly wilderness in the Highlands, revealing stunning mountain grandeur, breathtaking panoramas and horizons, tranquil lochs and moorland that riveted passengers.

The line from Glasgow takes a route that passes through Garelochhead, running up Loch Long to Arrochar, where it then cuts through to Tarbet on Loch Lomond side. It then follows the west bank of Loch Lomond north to Glen Falloch and Crianlarich, and on to Tyndrum, having passed through country familiar to Rob Roy MacGregor and the scene of Bruce's battle at Dail Righ.

Passing under the cone of Beinn Dorain, it reaches the station at Bridge of Orchy. The line then swings east, away from the more recent road, to cross the vast table land of Rannoch Moor, where some 10 miles is built on a 'floating' base to counteract the water-logged moorland.

After 87 miles, it reaches Rannoch Station – a destination familiar to many of the climbing fraternity – before swinging north-west through the lonely mountain country around Loch Treig. It reaches Spean Bridge 113.5 miles from Glasgow, before turning south-west, passing the ruins of Inverlochy Castle – built by the Comyn family in the 1200s, and scene of one of Montrose's great victories in later years. Finally it gets to Fort William, after 122.5 miles of stunning scenery and panoramic views.

Much of the fort that gave Fort William its name was demolished to make way for the railway station, having lain dormant since 1855. In 1896, two years after the railway was complete, the gateway from the original fort was re-erected at the Craigs, the town's old cemetery. Incidentally, that was the same year electricity was introduced to Fort William.

Permission was granted to extend the railway by Glenfinnan to Morar and Mallaig, in the hope of increasing business and general trade for the Hebrides. It also connected with the Caledonian Canal, running north-east to Inverness. Communication in the Highlands was improving by leaps and bounds.

Today, priorities have changed and the railway is used more for the transportation of tourists than the transportation of goods.

CHAPTER FORTY-THREE

The Home Rulers

Memorials to the men of courage and vision behind Scotland's move towards control of her own destiny.

THE 'HOME RULE' ERA of the late 19th and early 20th centuries was a time when many influential people believed the Union with England was having a negative effect on Scotland's national well-being. Amongst the most interesting characters demanding increased independence for Scotland was aristocrat, socialist, writer and adventurer Robert Bontine Cunninghame Graham. He was clearly a man of a few contradictions, but his key role in the emergence of nationalism and socialism in Scotland helped earn his place in Scottish history.

A year after Cunninghame Graham's death in 1936, a monument was erected to him on the outskirts of Dumbarton. It was moved to Gartmore in May 1981. This is only one of a long list of monuments erected to inspirational Scottish figures during the 'Home Rule' period.

The best known examples are those to William Wallace. The oldest surviving Wallace monument is the huge statue that stands on a wooded hillside above the River Tweed near the ruins of Dryburgh Abbey, the burial place of Sir Walter Scott. It was commissioned by the 11th Earl of Buchan and placed on its pedestal on 11 September 1814, the anniversary of Wallace's victory at Stirling Bridge in 1297. It was reported that: 'it occupies so eminent a situation, that Wallace, frowning towards England, can be seen from a distance of more than 30 miles.' The statue was originally painted white, but is today unpainted and unadorned in red sandstone. It stands near the village of St Boswells on the A68, which runs south through beautiful Border country.

The most famous of the Wallace monuments of this period is the

National Wallace Monument that stands atop the Abbey Craig, rising high above the River Forth near Stirling. The Abbey Craig (so called because of its proximity to the ruins of Cambuskenneth Abbey) was the site where Wallace and his co-commander, Murray, marshalled their troops before the battle of Stirling Bridge. Many battles have been fought in this vicinity, due to the fact that any invading army progressing northwards had to cross the Forth here, as it could not be bridged further east and the ground became too rough further west.

The monument was designed by J. T. Rochead, of Glasgow, in the form of a baronial tower 220ft high. As it stands upon the highest part of the Abbey Craig at 362ft, the view from the top is spectacular, the vista taking in the flood plain of the Forth, the distant Highland hills, and the fault line of the Ochils. The monument was founded on 24 June 1861, and completed in September 1869. But the official opening did not take place until 25 June 1887, when the statue of Wallace on a corner of the building was unveiled, finishing it to its original design. The whole structure cost £18,000. Standing before it today, and gazing up towards its baronial crown, eyes covering architecture conceived on a mighty scale, I wonder how much it would cost to create the equivalent now. Millions of pounds, I would imagine.

To help in its construction, a little railway line ran up the route of the modern approach, but this was removed after the building's completion. It would perhaps have been a good idea to have kept the line in position to transport visitors to the top. It would surely have added to the attraction of the site.

Many people assume that the current interest in Wallace is attributable to *Braveheart*, the 1995 motion picture, but it seems that he comes to the fore of the Scottish consciousness in cycles. When the foundation stone of the Abbey Craig monument was laid, 80,000 people turned out to see it – over 10 times the number that Wallace and Murray commanded on the day of battle! The fact that so many wished to be present at this occasion to mark Scotland's great hero belies the notion that our little nation had somehow been assimilated into the Victorian idea of 'Great Britain'. It seems many still had a very attuned sense of what it meant to be Scottish.

CHAPTER FORTY-FOUR

Golden days of steam

*Glasgow was the centre of the locomotive industry, with
more than 2,000 employed in the huge Springburn works.
Sadly they are now only a memory, but reminders of those
glory days remain.*

THINKING OF THE EMPIRE when it was at its height, I am reminded of
the time of the steam locomotive, and the network of railway lines
spreading across the face of the planet. Glasgow and Edinburgh
were first linked by railway in 1841–42. As the line approached
Glasgow's Queen Street Station, it went through a country village
named Springburn, and then began a long incline down through a
tunnel to take it beneath the Forth and Clyde canal.

It had originally been planned to take the new railway over the
top of the canal on a bridge and embankment, but this was success-
fully opposed by the canal owners, whose noses were possibly put
out of joint at the usurpation of their trade by these new-fangled
railways.

The tunnel took two and a half years to build, was dug by 500
men working in continuous shifts, and is still familiar to travellers
today. The present Edinburgh-Glasgow train runs through the tunnel's
darkness before it arrives at Queen Street's platforms.

The railway company purchased lands at the head of the incline
and constructed yards to build and repair locomotives. These
yards at Springburn were to develop, and eventually became the
biggest and greatest locomotive manufacturing centre outside the
United States.

In 1865, the Edinburgh and Glasgow Railway was taken over by
the North British Railway, and the works expanded to build more
powerful locomotives. In all, the Cowlairs works at Springburn
built a total of 850, which were shipped to every corner of the

globe. Ships on the Clyde carried them to such places as Belgium, Canada, Russia, Australia, South Africa and India. In fact, the last working loco from Springburn was a 19d-type, which until recently was in service at the Lorraine Gold Mine in South Africa.

The works themselves were at their height in 1895, when they were responsible not just for building, but also for maintaining locomotives, and their stock consisted of 800 engines, 2,755 coaches and more than 51,000 other rolling stock. The workforce numbered more than 2,000.

Old photos of the Cowlairs workforce always fascinate, as it is hard to find a member of staff not sporting a large flat cap at a jaunty angle. Near to the Cowlairs works stood the St Rollox works, which was the manufacturing base for the Caledonian Railway. These two were eventually amalgamated as the creep began towards nationalisation under British Rail.

Although the yards at Springburn are now just a memory, lost under the spread of modern housing, a few remnants can still be found. North Glasgow College in Springburn is housed in what was formerly the main office of the North British Railway. This building, at 110 Flemington Street, was designed by the architect James Miller, and was officially opened in 1909 by Lord Rosebery. Above the main entrance, a carving of a steam engine projects forward, as if bursting from the masonry. Flanking it are two statues, one representing 'Speed', with its figure sporting a flying cloak, and the other representing 'Science', holding a globe and compass. There are many other fixtures and fittings inside the building recalling its association with the North British, and leaflets giving a guide to these are available at reception at the main entrance. Nearby is the little Springburn Library and Museum, where information is available on the history of the district.

On the banks of the Clyde another relic of these days exists in the form of the giant Stobcross Crane, which most people seem to refer to as the Finnieston Crane, standing by the modern SECC building. This huge structure was constructed to lift the locomotives into the holds of waiting ships. Locomotives carried on low-loaders through the city streets were once a familiar sight in Glasgow, when the name of Scotland's largest city was synonymous with heavy industry.

CHAPTER FORTY-FIVE

The great exhibitions

They were spectacles of splendour; visitors arrived by the million and Glasgow benefited from the profits. Some of the legacies are still around.

IN THE LATE 1800s, when Britain was still at the height of its power on the world stage, Scotland decided to assert its role by staging exhibitions on a grand scale.

Quite a few of us will remember the Glasgow Garden Festival of 1988, complete with the giant Coca Cola rollercoaster on the banks of the Clyde, and the reappearance of the Glasgow trams – even if they did only run up and down a few hundred metres of track within the festival environs. In the few years since the Garden Festival, the site has changed hugely, with much development taking place there, in what was originally Glasgow's dockland.

The earlier festivals are largely forgotten – simply due to the ever-changing population – and the details are now just numbers in dusty archives interspersed with grainy black and white photographs. Nonetheless, they were huge successes and they catapulted Edinburgh, Glasgow and Scotland forward in the world.

Edinburgh had staged an international exhibition in 1886, but the first great Glasgow Exhibition, in 1888, the year Celtic FC was founded, was bigger by far than anything that had gone before.

The venue for this huge undertaking was the present Kelvingrove Park. Walking the paths today along the banks of the River Kelvin, it is difficult to picture the huge multi-coloured and exotic-looking pavilions that were constructed to emphasise Glasgow's status as 'Second City of the Empire'.

At the same time as plans for the exhibition were being drawn up, a competition was started to design a fitting City Chambers for Glasgow. The winning entry was, of course, today's impressive building overlooking George Square. But the runner-up also had his design put into construction by the Scottish Co-operative Society as its headquarters, and it stands hard alongside the Clyde at the south-east corner of the Kingston Bridge. This building has been converted into modern flats and apartments.

Glasgow was determined to show that it could be as lavish in its self-promotion as any other city in the world. The admission fee for the 1888 Exhibition was one shilling (five pence) and a total of 5,748,379 people passed through the turnstiles.

The profits were used to construct the Kelvingrove Art Gallery and Museum, which stands on part of the 1888 Exhibition grounds today. Admission to this gallery is free (although donations are always welcome), and the building itself is as much of an exhibit as any artefact on display within. Victorian opulence is evident in every view within the building, whether gazing up at the lofty ceilings, or from its galleries down to ground-floor level.

There is a strange urban myth prevalent in Glasgow, which I first heard as a child, that this gallery was accidentally constructed back to front, and the architect, on seeing the completed work, committed suicide in despair. This is not true, but it is such a widespread story that I would love to know its origin.

If you visit Kelvingrove Art Gallery and Museum, take a look at the bridge over the Kelvin a little east of the building, on Kelvin Way. There is a large bronze statue at each corner. The one on the north-east corner was struck by a bomb from a German aircraft during the Second World War and had to be reconstructed. A little plaque tells the story.

It was decided to mark the opening of Kelvingrove in 1901 by holding another great exhibition, and this one proved so popular that almost 11.5 million people attended. The pavilions were staggering in their splendour, the 'Industrial Hall' looking something like the ancient Hagia Sofia of Istanbul. Today nothing remains but the site, which, like that of the 1888 exhibition, is in the modern Kelvingrove Park.

We can only imagine the gondolas carrying passengers along the river, and the early rollercoaster rides, or 'switchbacks' as they were known, which were huge crowd-pullers. After all, these exhibitions were the Disneylands of their day.

A third great exhibition, the last to be held at Kelvingrove, took place in 1911, but it had a different, more distinctly Scottish theme than its predecessors.

The last great exhibition to be held before the dark days of the Second World War was at Bellahouston Park. This was the Empire Exhibition of 1938. One remnant survives – the Palace of Arts, a little reminder of the glory days of spellbinding exhibitions.

CHAPTER FORTY-SIX

Scotland's fine engineering heritage

*In 1913 more than one ship per day was launched
on the Clyde. Heavy industry flourished. Although the
glory days are over, many locations are lovingly maintained
as heritage sites.*

THE AFTERMATH OF THE First World War saw the collapse of industry in Britain. The statistics regarding tonnage of shipping launched on the Clyde before the Great War are quite remarkable. One fifth of the world's shipping bore the famous moniker 'Clyde-built' around the turn of the 20th century. 1913 saw an astonishing fact – more than one ship per day was launched on the Clyde during this vintage year.

Following the war came unrest, the General Strike, the Depression, but the Second World War saw a last sparkle before the days of the great shipyards became a distant memory. I remember the late Jack House, a great Glasgow 'expert', once state to an American audience how during the 1939–45 period, there was three times as much shipping launched on the Clyde as there was in every yard in the USA put together. He was jeered in disbelief.

The bulk of the old yards are now wasteland, or modern development has crept over their sites, but there are many other seats of industry that, fortunately, have been saved for future generations to enjoy and enable us to appreciate the days of Empire and prosperity.

The Bonawe Iron Furnace stands beside Loch Etive near Taynuilt on the A85, some 24 km east of Oban. It was economical in the 1700s to build this iron smelter here because of the availability of trees to make charcoal for the furnaces. The main complex is open to visitors, and is signposted from the main road.

While in Taynuilt, the railway station is well worth a visit. It is a typical Highland example, built in 1879, with the main offices on one platform with a detached signal box, and the small wooden shelter on the other.

Trains still run through, but the station itself is a preserved example of a bygone age. While on the theme of railways, the Glenfinnan viaduct, standing across the glen behind the monument to the '45, and the subject of many calendars and postcards, it is a lasting testament to the industry itself.

It was opened in 1901, part of the Fort William to Mallaig line. It has 21 spans covering a length of over a thousand feet, and the whole structure is made up of mass-concrete, an early example of what was then a new way of building.

The Lanarkshire village of Biggar, in Upper Clydesdale, still has its little gas works preserved and in the care of the Royal Museum of Scotland. These small town gas works were once familiar sights in Scotland, but this is one of the few surviving. It is signposted from the A702 running through the centre of Biggar.

Biggar has several museums all with different themes, quite extraordinary for a village of its size. Slightly further north stands the New Lanark industrial village in the banks of the Clyde, a mile south of Lanark itself. It is Scotland's outstanding monument to the Industrial Revolution, and a lasting memorial to the social reforms of David Dale and Robert Owen. A visit here is a day out in itself.

Coatbridge has the Summerlee Heritage Park, signposted from the surrounding motorway network. It is a museum dedicated to the former heavy industrialisation of the area and there is plenty to amuse both adults and children.

One of the major attractions is the system of trams that run on lines across the site, passing early locomotives. The tram drivers even stop to allow the kids to place pennies on the lines so they can be squashed like plasticine by the weight of the vehicles passing over them.

At the south end of Newtongrange on the A7 through Lothian stands the Lady Victoria Colliery, now run by the Scottish Mining Museum Trust. Standing over all is the famous symbol of the coal-fields, the pully wheels which raised and lowered the cages over

1,500 feet to the bases of the shafts far below. Inside the building stands the massive winding engine for the cables, built in Kilmarnock in 1894 and originally steam powered. It is now defunct, but lovingly looked after.

East of Musselburgh is the Prestongrange Beam-Engine and Brickworks, on the coast road on the southern shore of the Firth of Forth. The beam was constructed to drain the local mine of flood water and its very size impresses upon us the vast scale that 19th century engineers could work on, on these Lothian mines, as well as the Summerlee works which were once owned by the great Neilson family.

Over and above these are the ships, kept in a preserved state, which once sailed the seven seas, such as those at Dundee, where still stands the mighty railway bridge of the Tay and below, still jutting from the water, are the stumps from the fallen predecessor, a testimony to one of the greatest calamities of the age, the Tay Bridge disaster.

But remnants of the glory days are all around: the fine buildings in our cities, the great canals, the railways, the glass covered stations, and the bridges – the Forth railway bridge springs immediately to mind as a lasting testimony to times when Scotland and fine engineering went hand in hand.

CHAPTER FORTY-SEVEN

Scotland captured on Luftwaffe film

Many of the Scottish sites observed by the German Luftwaffe during the Second World War can still be found.

SCOTLAND HAD A VERY important role during the Second World War as a strategic stop-over for allied forces. A large number of airstrips, depots and naval bases sprouted up all over the country, from Wigtown to Lossiemouth, Benbecula to Orkney.

Throughout the period 1939–45, the German Luftwaffe took aerial photographs of sites all over Scotland as part of their war-time intelligence-gathering missions. With a little bit of detective work, many of these sites can still be seen today. Those who work at industrial estates, factories or hospitals, might relieve rush-hour traffic tedium by imagining the bustle of wartime activity that might once have taken place there.

Heathhall in Dumfries is now home to an industrial estate, but during the war it was an aircraft storage facility. Some of the arched hangars are still in use. In Lanarkshire, Carluke's Law Hospital was a military barracks. It was converted into a hospital after 1945 and continued with little change until fairly recently.

Scotland's coastline has inherited a vast legacy of relics from both the First and Second World Wars. Many present-day civilian airports and harbours have stories to tell. It is not hard to imagine, looking from the window of a plane or the observation deck of a ferry, the passing motion of an RAF Hurricane or a Royal Navy destroyer all those years ago.

At Longannet, near the Kincardine Bridge, 40 of the ammunition bunkers observed by Luftwaffe photographers in 1939 are still standing. The others were destroyed when the Longannet Power Station was built.

Montrose airfield in Angus has relics from the First World War.

Montrose is the oldest military airfield in Scotland, dating from 1912. It was home to No 2 Flying Instructors' School during the Second World War. A block of First World War aircraft sheds can be seen at the south-west corner of the airfield.

Those passing through Aberdeen International Airport might be interested to know that it was once home to RAF Dyce, occupied by Hurricanes of No 145 Squadron. A civil airport was first established there in 1934.

Moving up the coast, the Northern and Western Isles were of great strategic significance. They stand at the gateway between the North Atlantic, Arctic and the all-important Baltic. Easily accessible by ferry and plane today, the islands' war-time heritage provides a modern relief to earlier Gaelic and Norse heritage.

The Sullom Voe Oil terminal in Shetland is famous now for its prominence in Scotland's North Sea Oil industry, but during the Second World War the area was home to the Sullom Voe seaplane base, established to allow flying boats to patrol the seas from Norway to Iceland, upon which allied ships made precarious journeys above the watchful eyes of the German U-boat commanders.

The airfield on the small Outer Hebridean island of Benbecula was originally a civilian airport, but was developed under the auspices of Coastal Command for anti-submarine patrols in the North Atlantic. The military connection is still very much in evidence today, as the airport now serves the Rocket Range on the neighbouring island of South Uist.

CHAPTER FORTY-EIGHT

Hydro dams bring new life

The hydro-electricity schemes transformed Scotland and its image after the Second World War, in a mixture of power and spectacle.

STANDING HIGH ABOVE the main road running west from Tyndrum to Oban stands the Cruachan Dam, nestling in the great corrie of Ben Cruachan, 3,689ft. Cruachan is one of the classic ascents of the Munros of Scotland, which most climbers are eager to add to their list. It was the scene of one of Robert the Bruce's early victories.

But it is deep within the mountain itself that the biggest surprise awaits – a mini-bus drive two-thirds of a mile into the rock, where a cavern 300ft long, 77ft wide and 127ft high is hewn from the solid granite.

There are four huge turbines, each weighing 650 tons, which can pump 120 tons of water a second, sitting 1,000ft beneath the Cruachan Dam, and 120ft beneath the level of Loch Awe. When demand is low, the turbines pump water up into the dam, and when demand is high, the water flows down to drive the turbines and generate power for Scotland's grid.

Cruachan Power Station is open to visitors from late April till late September. The dam high above is noted for its spectacular views. There is an access road that runs to it from Lochawe village, where you can park. The walk is three and a half miles, and you can enjoy an ever-changing panorama south over the loch and north to Cruachan's serrated peaks.

The dam is 1,037ft long and 153ft high, containing 116,000 cubic yards of concrete. It stands 1,315ft above sea level. Cruachan generates more electricity than the nuclear power station of Hunterston in Ayrshire.

There are extensive hydro-electric developments in the area surrounding Pitlochry. The town holds the Clunie Memorial arch, which is built in the same shape as the huge tunnels underground that carry the water. It was built to mark the completion of the dramatic Tummel-Garry hydro scheme in 1952.

There are generating stations at Pitlochry and Clunie, and west of Pitlochry main street stands the 54ft-high Pitlochry Dam. A salmon ladder has been constructed so that the fish can bypass the dam to reach their original spawning grounds. Observation windows allow visitors to watch the fish ascend, and they have become great tourist attractions, particularly when the salmon are running. The building of Pitlochry Dam created a new loch – Loch Faskally, which is crossed by a bridge carrying the A9.

A road runs from Tayside up to the visitor centre at Ben Lawers, which at 3,984ft is the highest mountain in Perthshire. Continuing northwards past the visitor centre, heading towards the pass over to Bridge of Balgie in Glen Lyon, you soon come across the dam that holds back the waters of Lochan na Lairige, the Loch of the Pass. This is one of my favourite wee dams, with Lawers towering on the right, and the Tarmachan Range rising on the left to 3,421ft.

Still in Perthshire are the twin dams of Lyon and Giorra at the head of Glen Lyon, the longest and one of the most beautiful glens in Scotland, which has a display of spectacular colours in autumn.

There is an extensive hydro-electric system based around Loch Quoich, accessible from the A87, which runs westwards from the Great Glen, but the raised water levels and deforestation have taken away some of the original glories of this wilderness.

Another accessible dam is the one at the south end of Loch Glascarnoch on the A835 north to Ullapool.

Close to the central belt of Scotland, there is the artificially-enlarged Carron Valley Reservoir, in the valley of the same name, running between Fintry and Denny, and traversed by the B818. This example is unusual, having a large dam at either end of the loch, the easternmost giving off the River Carron and the other the Endrick Water. The site of the loch was originally owned by Sir John the Graham, who died fighting alongside Wallace at the Battle of Falkirk, and the remains of Sir John's castle stand above the dam at the western end of the loch.

CHAPTER FORTY-NINE

Read the story of Scotland

If you don't know the past then you cannot read the future. But fortunately there have never been so many good books on Scotland.

AT SCHOOL I WAS taught history from the English point of view. Like everyone in Scotland, when asked: 'When was the Battle of Hastings?' I could immediately reply: '1066'. I also learned about the Wars of the Roses and the Magna Carta. None of these topics had anything to do with Scotland. The martyrdom of Wallace and the astonishing achievements of Bruce's reign were quickly skimmed over.

When I left school, I discovered the books of the late Nigel Tranter, and with over a hundred titles by the man, my voracious appetite for reading them was rewarded by a grounding in what had actually occurred in Scotland's past.

Tranter made me want to read academic history texts, and I would do so whenever I discovered them. I moved on to other writers who wrote in a particularly Scottish vein; John Prebble for instance. I mention this because I write constantly, and I tend to write about places to visit in our little country, but Scotland, the country, and Scotland's history, are inextricably intertwined.

We may live in a technological age, but the landscape of our nation is still discernably the same as that which Calgacus knew, which Wallace and Bruce knew, which Tranter knew. The Southern Uplands and the Borderland are still laid out as the reivers knew it, and the Tweed still runs as it did when the army of James IV crossed en route to the disaster of Flodden. The central belt has its battle sites, like Bannockburn and Stirling Bridge, and in the north the glens where Charles Edward Stewart hid from pursuing Hanoverians still stand basically unchanged.

What has changed in the past few decades is the interest in and understanding of our past. Writers like Tranter opened up our national memory, and our historic abbeys, castles, battle sites and birthplaces are teeming with visitors like never before. The mountain country has opened up and many thousands now take to the hills for recreation.

There are only five million people living in Scotland today, but Tranter's books are familiar to many more. They are opening up Scotland to a much wider audience, such as those of Scots ancestry in the Americas and Australia.

A knowledge of our past lets us know where we are going: how do you know your destination if you don't know where you left from? And it is fact that in the latter half of the 20th century so many books emerged covering every aspect of Scotland's culture that they could only serve to educate people about the country.

As a writer, I make many appearances in bookshops to do talks and slide shows, and I hear the staff say again and again that over the past few years history books have just flown off the shelves.

The film *Braveheart* helped dramatically. Many were quick to point out its inaccuracies, but it started a rush to learn more, and that can only be a good thing. It brought Wallace to a new generation. The knock-on effect of all this is the Scottish Parliament. Increased awareness brought on increased calls for its return.

Knowledge is power. So do yourself a favour and visit some of our historic attractions. They are part of the living, breathing fabric of Scotland. Skara Brae in Orkney, the Buchanan Galleries Shopping Centre in Glasgow and everywhere in between; all are part of our ever-changing idea of architecture. Great castles like Stirling or Edinburgh, although ancient, are still in use to this day, and we should not forget the major players in all this history business – the people.

I feel as though the blood that runs in my veins is the same as that which ran in the men who backed Calgacus against the might of the Roman invaders. That same blood was there at Stirling Bridge, Bannockburn and a host of other fights where Scotland struggled for its right to exist.

READ THE STORY OF SCOTLAND

I suppose I'm trying to say that the best site with a connection to Scotland's history I can recommend in this section is your nearest library or bookshop. It's all there.

CHAPTER FIFTY

Scotland is the star

*A look behind some well-known Scottish films to find
their wondrous and varied locations.*

I'VE ALWAYS LOVED Scotland-based films. *Whisky Galore* and its
follow-up *Rockets Galore*, made in the Western Isles. Tranter's novel,
Bridal Path, became a film, which had its premiere in Scotland. I
especially liked the Highlander in the lead role, who, although lost,
refused to admit that any Highlander could be lost anywhere in the
country north of Loch Lomond.

The Maggie, a story of a puffer – very much in the *Para Handy*
mould – was an absolute delight. I enjoyed seeing the boat stuck on
the roof of the Glasgow Underground underneath the suspension
bridge on the Clyde.

These films all have a similar streak. They all have a particularly
Scottish gentle humour. This humour has continued on in our films
up to recent times.

It was apparent in *Gregory's Girl*. I have often seen it erroneously
stated that *Gregory's Girl* was filmed in East Kilbride, when it was
actually filmed in Cumbernauld. One memorable scene is John
Gordon Sinclair waiting for Dee Hepburn. He is obviously being
stood up and he just happens to be standing in front of a huge
clock. That clock was mounted on the wall of the shopping centre
in Cumbernauld.

Bill Forsyth, director of *Gregory's Girl*, went on to make *Local
Hero*, another film with a very Scottish flavour of tongue firmly in
cheek humour. The beach scenes were filmed on the famous silver
sands to the south of Mallaig at Morar. The beaches here are fan-
tastic – if only we had Mediterranean sun to go with them!

The village scenes were filmed at the other side of Scotland
at Pennan, a picturesque little fishing port close to the boundary

of Aberdeenshire and Banff. The village phone box, which figures so prominently in the film, is a magnet for visitors taking photographs.

More recently there have been Hollywood blockbusters such as *Rob Roy*, starring Liam Neeson. From the first scenes, the splendid scenery of Scotland is evident, the opening shots taken above Loch Leven to the north of Glencoe. Rob Roy's adversary, the Marquis of Montrose, played by John Hurt, lives in remarkable splendour. Drummond Castle near Crieff was used for these shots. Although the castle itself is a private home, the landscaped gardens are open to the public at certain times.

The biggest film ever made with a Scottish theme has to be *Braveheart*, starring Mel Gibson as William Wallace.

People did take exception to an Australian playing Scotland's great hero, but he is an actor after all. Ben Kingsley played Gandhi, but I don't recall hearing a great outcry about that. Perhaps Wallace is a bit too close to the soul of many Scots.

The opening shots for *Braveheart* were filmed in Glen Nevis, running inland from Fort William. The famous mountain-top scene was filmed on the summit of Aonach Mor, close to Ben Nevis in the Lochaber mountain range.

The battle scenes were recorded in Ireland, which caused no end of controversy. The facts behind this are very simple. Scotland, having no control over its monetary affairs, was not able to offer better costs for the production crew, while Ireland, with its booming independent economy, was able to put together an attractive package for the film makers – offering the services of members of the Irish Territorial Army as extras in the battle scenes.

It was an opportunity missed for Scotland. I can however state that all the close battle shots were of Scots, showing a martial throwback inherent since medieval times!

While on the subject of Mel Gibson, his *Hamlet* was shot in Scotland. Dunnottar Castle, just south of Stonehaven, provided the backdrop for that particular film.

Highlander, in my view a classic film, released in 1989 and starring

Christopher Lambert and Sean Connery, featured Glen Coe in the battle scene. Glen Coe was also the site of Connor's tower, with the Three Sisters mountains prominent in the background.

Eilean Donan Castle figures prominently. Eilean Donan stands facing Loch Duich, by the village of Dornie in Ross-shire, and is open to the public from Easter to October. It also starred in the film *Loch Ness*, starring Ted Danson of *Cheers* fame.

The Cuillin Mountains of Skye also featured in *Highlander*, with one sword fight taking place on the famous Cioch, a curious jutting rock on a shoulder of Sgurr Alisdair. Skye was also the setting for the film *Dragonslayer*, a Disney product, the primeval landscape being ideally suited for such a title.

And speaking of Disney, who can forget *Greyfriars Bobby*, a film fortunately re-released on DVD? The Grassmarket in Edinburgh features, as does Edinburgh Castle and, of course, Greyfriars Church itself. Just opposite the churchyard gates is the statue to Bobby and I can recall seeing Walt Disney's signature on a wall of the Greyfriars Bobby's Bar, which stands next door.

Various parts of Scotland have appeared in the Harry Potter films. The grounds of Hogwarts school were filmed in the dramatic scenery of Glen Coe, and the flying car scene was filmed at Glenfinnan viaduct, just by the spot where Bonnie Prince Charlie raised the standard in 1745.

CHAPTER FIFTY-ONE

The dawning of a new era

11 SEPTEMBER 1997 was an auspicious day in Scotland's story. The people voted overwhelmingly for the reconvening of a parliament in Scotland. Only one area voted against Scotland taking this step forward, and that was Dumfries and Galloway. This should not really have been a surprise, as when I travel the highways and byways of that area I am always surprised at the number of English incomers I stumble across. Dumfries and Galloway is just over the Border from England, and many people from the south want to come and settle there. But I have always found it a little unfair that English people living in Scotland have the ability to vote for Unionist political parties, whereas Scots in England do not have the luxury of voting for a purely Scottish oriented party, and so incomers have the ability to vote on what is a Scottish issue and influence the outcome.

11 September was already an important date in our long story before the late 20th century. Wallace's great victory over the English at Stirling Bridge had been fought on that day in 1297. So it must have been a little more than coincidence that the day that Scotland was going to decide its constitutional future happened to be the 700th anniversary of Wallace's victory – to the day!

When the dust had settled and the votes were counted, Donald Dewar, Scotland's future first First Minister, called the outcome, 'the settled will of the Scottish people'.

There had been pushes to try to get Scotland her own parliament before of course, but the time had finally come when it was a reality and no longer a pipe dream. The parliament has curtailed powers – it cannot raise taxes or control Scotland's immigration policy, amongst other things, but most Scots see it as a step in the right direction.

Arguments began almost instantly. Scots would not be Scots if there were not a debate involved! Where should the new parliament building be situated? How much was it going to cost? When Holyrood was announced as the location, many were not happy. Many thought it should be sited on top of Calton Hill, somewhere that folk could look up to, rather than in a dip, hidden away at the base of the Royal Mile. The original costs were estimated somewhere between 10 and 40 million pounds, but costs escalated out of control and the finished product cost 430 million pounds. As there are only five million inhabitants of Scotland, the price to each and every one of us is apparent. The cost was so great that an enquiry was held, and the outcome of that enquiry criticised the management of the whole project.

Another factor that galled was the choice of a Catalan architect's design. Many Scots would rather have had a Scottish designer create their parliament building. It did not help that the architect died before work was finished, and changes were made to the design while work was underway. On top of this, the building was scheduled to open in 2001, and it was 2004 before it was actually finished.

But it is not all doom and gloom. The interior is impressive, and modern technology is used to the utmost. The people of Scotland and their politicians familiarly call the place 'Holyrood', so it has become part of them and what they are in a short space of time.

There are 129 Members of the Scottish Parliament, or MSPs as they are commonly known. 73 are elected by the 'first past the post' system, and the other 56 are chosen by a form of proportional representation.

There seems to have been a reawakening in Scotland over the last decade. Scots are finding their way forward with a new realisation of who and what they are – a distinctive people with their own cultural identity and sense of nationality. Having a parliament in their capital city helps to categorise this to some extent; something uniquely Scottish.

We have seen changes in this last decade that will be something future generations of Scots will read about in their history books. Scotland is an ongoing story. She evolves through the years, and her generations continue.

We are all linked in Scotland, each generation. There are many millions long gone who were able to take pride in the fact that they were Scots, and there are many millions still to come who will bear that moniker with that same pride.

Surely this small nation that has done so much on a world scale will one day take her rightful place on that planet, a proud independent people with a proud independent nation to match.

Some other books published by **LUATH** PRESS

On The Trail of Robert the Bruce

David R. Ross

ISBN 0 946487 52 9 PBK £7.99

This book from Scots historian David R. Ross charts the story of Scotland's hero-king from his boyhood, through his days of indecision as Scotland suffered under the English yoke, to his assumption of the crown exactly six months after the death of William Wallace. Here is the astonishing blow by blow account of how, against fearful odds, Bruce led the Scots to win their greatest ever victory. Bannockburn was not the end of the story. The war against English oppression lasted another 14 years. Bruce lived just long enough to see his dreams of an independent Scotland come to fruition in 1328 with the signing of the Treaty of Edinburgh. The trail takes us to Bruce sites in Scotland, many of the little known and forgotten battle sites in northern England, and as far afield as the Bruce monuments in Andalusia and Jerusalem.

- 67 places to visit in Scotland and elsewhere
- One general map, three location maps and a map of Bruce-connected sites in Ireland
- Bannockburn battle plan
- Drawings and reproductions of rarely seen illustrations

On the Trail of Robert the Bruce is not all blood and gore. It brings out the love and laughter, pain and passion of one of the great eras of Scottish history. Read it and you will understand why David R. Ross has never knowingly killed a spider in his life. Once again, he proves himself a master of the popular brand of hands-on history that made *On the Trail of William Wallace* so popular.

On the Trail of William Wallace

David R. Ross

ISBN 0 946487 47 2 PBK £7.99

On the Trail of William Wallace offers a refreshing insight into the life and heritage of the great Scots hero whose proud story is at the very heart of what it means to be Scottish, and whose effect on the ordinary Scot through the ages is manifest in the many sites where his memory is marked.

In trying to piece together the jigsaw of the reality of William Wallace's life, David R. Ross' book, *On the Trail of William Wallace*, weaves a subtle flow of new information with his own observations. His engaging, thoughtful and at times amusing narrative reads with the ease of a historical novel, complete with all the intrigue, treachery and romance required to hold the attention of the casual reader and still entice the more knowledgeable historian.

- 74 places to visit in Scotland and the north of England
- Stirling Bridge and Falkirk battle plans
- Wallace's route through London
- Wallace connections in North America and elsewhere

On the Trail of William Wallace will be enjoyed by anyone with an interest in Scotland, from the passing tourist to the most fervent nationalist. It is an encyclopedia-cum-guide book, literally stuffed with fascinating titbits not usually on offer in the conventional history books.

The biker-historian's unique combination of unabashed romanticism and easy irreverence make him the ideal guide to historical subjects.

THE SCOTSMAN

On the Trail of Bonnie Prince Charlie

David R. Ross

ISBN 0 946487 68 5 PBK £7.99

On the Trail of Bonnie Prince Charlie is the story of the Young Pretender. Born in Italy, grandson of James VII, at a time when the German house of Hanover was on the throne, his father was regarded by many as the rightful king. Bonnie Prince Charlie's campaign to retake the throne in his father's name changed the fate of Scotland. The Jacobite movement was responsible for the '45 Uprising, one of the most decisive times in Scottish history. The suffering following the battle of Culloden in 1746 still evokes emotion. Charles' own journey immediately after Culloden is well known: hiding in the heather, escaping to Skye with Flora MacDonald. Little is known of his return to London in 1750 incognito, where he converted to Protestantism (he reconverted to Catholicism before he died and is buried in the Vatican). He was often unwelcome in Europe after the failure of the uprising and came to hate any mention of Scotland and his lost chance.

Yet again popular historian David R. Ross brings his own style to one of Scotland's most famous figures. Bonnie Prince Charlie is part of the folklore of Scotland. He brings forth feelings of antagonism from some and romanticism from others, but all agree on his legal right to the throne.

Knowing the story behind the place can bring the landscape to life. Take this book with you on your travels and follow the route taken by Charles' forces on their doomed march.

Ross writes with an immediacy, a dynamism, that makes his subjects come alive on the page.

DUNDEE COURIER

A Passion for Scotland

David R. Ross

ISBN 1 84282 019 2 PBK £9.99

Eschewing xenophobia, his deep understanding of how Scotland's history touches her people shines through. All over Scotland, into England and Europe, over to Canada, Chicago and Washington – the people and the places that bring Scotland's story to life, and death – including

- Wallace and Bruce
- The Union Montrose
- The Jacobites
- John MacLean
- Tartan Day USA

and, revealed for the first time, the burial places of all Scotland's monarchs.

This is not a history book. But it covers history.

This is not a travel guide. But some places mentioned might be worth a visit.

This is not a political manifesto. But a personal one.

Read this book. It might make you angry. It might give you hope. You might shed a tear. You might not agree with David R. Ross.

But read this book. You might rediscover your roots, your passion for Scotland.

David R. Ross is passionate about Scotland's past, and its future. In this heartfelt journey through Scotland's story, he shares his passion for what it means to be a Scot, tackling the Act of Union, the Jacobite rebelion and revealing, for the first time, the final resting places of all Scotland's Kings and Queens.

A Passion for Scotland sounds a clarion call to Scots worldwide to revive genuine patriotism.

SCOTTISH TOURIST GUIDE

For Freedom

David R. Ross
ISBN 1 905222 28 9 PBK £9.99

David R. Ross, The 'Biker Historian', goes *On The Trail of William Wallace* again to investigate his last days, the events that led up to his death, and their repercussions through Scottish history. He ties Wallace's life and death to the issues of patriotism and Scottish nationality over the last 700 years, and identifies Wallace as a 'Scottish Martyr' who died for freedom and identity in the country he loved.

Desire Lines: A Scottish Odyssey

David R. Ross
ISBN 1 84282 033 8 PBK £9.99

David R. Ross not only shows us his Scotland but he teaches us it too. You feel as though you are on the back of his motorcycle listening to the stories of his land as you fly with him up and down the smaller roads, the 'desire lines', of Scotland. Ross takes us off the beaten track and away from the main routes chosen for us by modern road builders.

He starts our journey in England and criss-crosses the border telling the bloody tales of the towns and villages. His recounting of Scottish history, its myths and its legends is unapologetically and unashamedly pro-Scots.

His tour takes us northwards towards Edinburgh through Athelstaneford, the place where the Saltire was born. From there we head to the Forth valley and on into the Highlands and beyond, taking in the stories of the villains and heroes through Scottish history.

... an entertainingly outspoken companion for any inquisitive traveller round this nation ...
THE HERALD

David Ross is a passionate patriot. He is not afraid of stating his opinion, and he does so with unabashed gusto. The result is an enlightening travel book. But beware, it may tempt you on to a motorbike ...
SCOTS MAGAZINE

On the Trail of Scotland's Myths and Legends

Stuart McHardy

ISBN 1 84282 049 4 PBK £7.99

A journey through Scotland's past from the earliest times through the medium of the awe-inspiring stories that were at the heart our ancestors' traditions and beliefs.

As the art of storytelling bursts into new flower, many tales are being told again as they once were. As *On the Trail of Scotland's Myths and Legends* unfolds, mythical animals, supernatural beings, heroes, giants and goddesses come alive and walk Scotland's rich landscape as they did in the time of the Scots, Gaelic and Norse speakers of the past.

Visiting over 170 sites across Scotland, Stuart McHardy traces the lore of our ancestors, connecting ancient beliefs with traditions still alive today. Presenting a new picture of who the Scots are and where they have come from, this book provides an insight into a unique tradition of myth, legend and folklore that has marked the language and landscape of Scotland.

This is a revised and updated edition of Stuart McHardy's popular *Highland Myths and Legends*.

This remains an entertaining record of the extent to which history is memorialised in the landscape.

THE SCOTSMAN

The Quest for the Celtic Key

Karen Ralls-MacLeod and Ian Robertson

ISBN 1 84282 031 1 PBK £8.99

Full of mystery, magic and intrigue, Scotland's past is still burning with unanswered questions. Many of these have been asked before, some have never before been broached – but all are addressed with the inquisitiveness of true detectives in *The Quest for the Celtic Key*.

- Was Winston Churchill really a practising member of a Druid order?
- What are the similarities between Merlin and Christ?
- Did Arthur, king of the Britons, conquer Scotland and was he buried in Govan?
- Were the 3,500 year-old tartan-wearing mummies in China's Takla Makan desert Scottish?
- What is hidden in the vaults at Rosslyn Chapel?
- Why is the lore surrounding Scottish freemasonry so unique?

Encompassing well-known events and personae – such as Robert the Bruce, William Wallace, the Declaration of Arbroath and the Stone of Destiny – whilst also tackling the more obscure elements in Scottish history, the significance of the number 19, the power of the colour green and the spiritual meaning of locations across Scotland, *The Quest for the Celtic Key* illustrates how the seemingly disparate 'mysteries of history' are connected.

The Quest for Arthur

Stuart McHardy

ISBN 1 84282 012 5 HBK £16.99

 King Arthur of Camelot and the Knights of the Round Table are enduring romantic figures. A national hero for the Britons, the Welsh and the English alike, Arthur is a potent figure for many. This quest leads to a radical new knowledge of the ancient myth.

Historian, storyteller and folklorist Stuart McHardy believes he has uncovered the origins of this inspirational figure, the true Arthur. He incorporates knowledge of folklore and placename studies with an archaeological understanding of the sixth century.

Combining knowledge of the earliest records and histories of Arthur with an awareness of the importance of oral traditions, this quest leads to the discovery that the enigmatic origins of Arthur lie not in Brittany, England or Wales. Instead they lie in that magic land the ancient Welsh called Y Gogledd, 'The North', the North of Britain, which we now call – Scotland.

(Stuart McHardy's) findings are set to shake established Arthurian thinking
THE SCOTSMAN

Reportage Scotland: History in the Making

Louise Yeoman

Foreword by Professor David Stevenson

ISBN 1 84282 051 6 PBK £6.99

 Events – both major and minor – as seen and recorded by Scots throughout history.

- Which king was murdered in a sewer? What was Dr Fian's love magic?
- Who was the half-roasted abbot?
- Which cardinal was salted and put in a barrel?
- Why did Lord Kitchener's niece try to blow up Burns's cottage?

The answers can all be found in the eclectic mix covering nearly 2000 years of Scottish history. Historian Louise Yeoman's rummage through the manuscript, book and newspapers archives of the National Library of Scotland has yielded an astonishing amount of material. Ranging from a letter to the King of the Picts to Mary Queen of Scots' own account of the murder of David Riccio; from the execution of William Wallace to accounts of anti-poll tax actions and the opening of the new Scottish Parliament. The book takes pieces from the original French, Latin, Gaelic and Scots and makes them accessible to the general reader, often for the first time.

The result is compelling reading for anyone interested in the history that has made Scotland what it is today.

The Price of Scotland: Darien, Union and the Wealth of Nations

Douglas Watt

ISBN: 1 906307 09 1 PBK £9.99

The attempt by the Company of Scotland to establish a colony at Darien in Central America is one of the best known episodes in late 17th century Scottish history. The catastrophic failure of the scheme, one of Scotland's worst losses, was followed a few years later by the Treaty of Union in 1707 which dissolved the Company and ended the existence of the Scottish Parliament.

Douglas Watt charts the Darien Scheme from its inception to its demise against the financial background of the period, looking at previously unexamined evidence and considering both the political and financial implications of this key moment in history.
The Price of Scotland provides a fresh examination and timely re-assessment of Scotland's strange journey from Darien to the Wealth of Nations, from Nation State to Stateless Nation.

It is this mess [the state of Scotland at the time of Union] to which Douglas Watt has brought an economist's eye and poet's sensibility in The Price of Scotland... to show definitively... that over-ambition and mismanagement, rather than English mendacity, doomed Scotland's imperial ambitions.

Ruaridh Nicoll, THE OBSERVER

The Price of Scotland treats Darien as a financial mania.

FINANCIAL TIMES

Caledonia's Last Stand: in search of the lost Scots of Darien

Nat Edwards

ISBN 1 905222 84 X PBK £12.99

History alone could not explain the colony's disastrous outcome; you really had to stand on the shore of Punta Escoces to realise that the Scots were bound to disaster the moment they chose the site of the settlement they christened Caledonia. The bay was a beautiful, deadly trap.

NAT EDWARDS

On 2 November 1698 a fleet landed in the Isthmus of Darien to create a colony and launch a new Scottish trading empire. The venture failed dramatically, with a catastrophic loss of life and money, and led to the eventual end of Scottish independence and the beginning of the UK.

Nat Edwards' erratic odyssey to find the graves of the Scots settlers is a reflection of the story of the Scots Company itself, interweaving pirates, street riots, treasure hunters, indigenous peoples and killer bees with the astonishing facts of Darien. Panama is the real-life setting for an almost unbelievable 17th century of Scottish hope and adventure, and Nat Edwards' discoveries are often frustrating, occasionally freakish, but always fascinating.

Scots in the USA

Jenni Calder

ISBN 1 905222 06 8   PBK £8.99

The map of the United States is peppered with Scottish place-names and America's telephone directories are filled with surnames illustrating Scottish ancestry. Increasingly, Americans of Scottish extraction are visiting Scotland in search of their family history. All over Scotland and the United States there are clues to the Scottish-American relationship, the legacy of centuries of trade and communication as well as that of departure and heritage.

The experiences of Scottish settlers in the United States varied enormously, as did their attitudes to the lifestyles that they left behind and those that they began anew once they arrived in North America.

Scots in the USA discusses why they left Scotland, where they went once they reached the United States, and what they did when they got there.

... a valuable readable and illuminating addition to a burgeoning literature... should be required reading on the flight to New York by all those on the Tartan Week trail.

SUNDAY HERALD

Scots in Canada

Jenni Calder

ISBN 1 84282 038 9   PBK £7.99

The story of the Scots who went to Canada, from the 17th century onwards.

In Canada there are nearly as many descendants of Scots as there are people living in Scotland; almost five million Canadians ticked the 'Scottish origin' box in the most recent Canadian Census. Many Scottish families have friends or relatives in Canada.

Thousands of Scots were forced from their homeland, while others chose to leave, seeking a better life. As individuals, families and communities, they braved the wild Atlantic Ocean, many crossing in cramped under-rationed ships, unprepared for the fierce Canadian winter. And yet Scots went on to lay railroads, found banks and exploit the fur trade, and helped form the political infrastructure of modern day Canada.

... meticulously researched and fluently written... it neatly charts the rise of a country without succumbing to sentimental myths

SCOTLAND ON SUNDAY

Luath Press Limited

committed to publishing well written books worth reading

LUATH PRESS takes its name from Robert Burns, whose little collie Luath (*Gael.,* swift or nimble) tripped up Jean Armour at a wedding and gave him the chance to speak to the woman who was to be his wife and the abiding love of his life. Burns called one of 'The Twa Dogs' Luath after Cuchullin's hunting dog in Ossian's *Fingal*. Luath Press was established in 1981 in the heart of Burns country, and now resides a few steps up the road from Burns' first lodgings on Edinburgh's Royal Mile. Luath offers you distinctive writing with a hint of unexpected pleasures.

Most bookshops in the UK, the US, Canada, Australia, New Zealand and parts of Europe either carry our books in stock or can order them for you. To order direct from us, please send a £sterling cheque, postal order, international money order or your credit card details (number, address of cardholder and expiry date) to us at the address below. Please add post and packing as follows: UK – £1.00 per delivery address; overseas surface mail – £2.50 per delivery address; overseas airmail – £3.50 for the first book to each delivery address, plus £1.00 for each additional book by airmail to the same address. If your order is a gift, we will happily enclose your card or message at no extra charge.

Luath Press Limited
543/2 Castlehill
The Royal Mile
Edinburgh EH1 2ND
Scotland
Telephone: 0131 225 4326 (24 hours)
Fax: 0131 225 4324
email: sales@luath.co.uk
Website: www.luath.co.uk

ILLUSTRATION: IAN KELLAS